"Taylor chronicles biblical accounts of God teaching His people to be relentless. Each intriguing story will draw you in and captivate your attention. Readers immerse themselves in the struggles of every character and emerge bound and determined to hang tough in the face of any obstacle. I needed this book. I will reach for it time and time again for instruction and inspiration."

—Sandy Wisdom-Martin, executive director-treasurer, National WMU, coauthor of *On the Journey*

"You will never be able to look at the familiar and beloved characters in the Bible in quite the same way after reading *Relentless.* Taylor Field gives remarkable twenty-first century insight into the men and women who sought and found God through the pages of biblical history. You will discover the many ways you share the same emotions and responses that Moses, Ruth, Jacob, and Peter experienced. And you will realize anew the remarkable resources available to you as you relentlessly pursue His path for *your* journey."

—Rosalie Hall Hunt, daughter of missionaries to China, served as an IMB missionary in eight countries of Asia, member of the board of the WMU Foundation, and author of numerous books about missions pioneers, including *Bless God and Take Courage: The Judson History and Legacy*

"Taylor Field has done it again. In his familiar and insightful way, he has retold numerous stories from the Bible that seemingly had little connection to me. And yet, now I see parts of my life in every chapter of his new book, *Relentless: The Path to Holding On*. I especially love how he begins and ends his book with different applications of the same biblical story. And he has cast a new light on my favorite story of the paralyzed man whose friends lowered him through the roof so Jesus could heal him. The reader will be challenged in every chapter to prove that we are as relentless in our faith as those who came before us and showed us the way."

—David George, president, WMU Foundation

"Perhaps the greatest thing any pastor can accomplish is helping a person hear the voice of God. Through his life, ministry, and writing Taylor has consistently been a shepherd that has helped me know the Shepherd's voice. Taylor has a unique ability to tell stories—curated either from his personal experiences serving on the gritty streets of the Lower East Side or from prolific sources as a voracious reader. *Relentless*, however, is unique. The stories are nothing new; after all, they are stories of men and women found in the Bible. Yet, somehow as I read these stories of characters I've known since my childhood, they became real; in fact, they became me."

—Andrew Mann, director, Graffiti 2 Community Ministries, author of *Upside-Down Joy*

"Clear and moving reminders that the most impressive miracles of the Bible are the miracles of faith enough to stick to it."

—Travis Collins, pastor, First Baptist Church of Huntsville, Alabama, author of *Directionally Challenged*, *Tough Calls*, and *What Does it Mean to be Welcoming?*

"Taylor is a gifted communicator who continually challenges me in all his writings. Whether it be the Upside-Down series, *Mercy Streets*, or *The Wayward Way*, I finish each book wanting more. *Relentless* is no exception. It challenges me to keep going when the going gets tough."

—Kristy Carr, senior manager, National WMU

Relentless

The Path to Holding On

Taylor Field

NEW HOPE®
PUBLISHERS
Imprint of Iron Stream Media

Birmingham, Alabama

Other New Hope Books by Taylor Field

Upside-Down Devotion: Extreme Action for a Remarkable God
Upside-Down Freedom: Inverted Principles for Christian Living
Upside-Down Leadership: Rethinking Influence and Success
The Wayward Way: The Power in Wilderness Journeys

New Hope® Publishers
100 Missionary Ridge
Birmingham, AL 35242
An imprint of Iron Stream Media
NewHopePublishers.com
IronStreamMedia.com

All italicized Scripture are made by the author of the book for emphasis. The chapters are personal reflections on what biblical entities could be thinking in relation to being relentless and are not intended as doctrinal statements.

Library of Congress Cataloging-in-Publication Data has been filed.

ISBN-13: 978-1-56309-355-5
Ebook ISBN: 978-1-56309-356-2

1 2 3 4 5—24 23 22 21 20

To those who hold on and to those who give in

To the Reader

About the cover of *Relentless*

I am fascinated with the story of Jacob wrestling with God (or an angel); what a remarkable experience for a human being, this one human being. It happened at night when he moved his family off to the other side of the river and was left alone. The struggle would last until almost daybreak. There are so many ways to view this story metaphorically and literally. I wanted this piece to capture the darkness that enveloped Jacob that night. I believe it represents the darkness we feel when we are struggling. Just like with Jacob though, there is always hope. The splash of lighter colors in contrast to the darkness and the expanse of the night sky is intended to remind people that hope surrounds them.

We all have our struggles—we all have something that we want dearly. Hope is there for those who are in the struggle.

—Chris Cook, artist

But we're not quitters who lose out. Oh, no! We'll stay with it and survive, trusting all the way.

—Hebrews 10:39 The Message

But we do not belong to those who shrink back and are destroyed, but to those who have faith and are saved.

—Hebrews 10:39 NIV

Contents

Resilience

Child

You're five years old. He is as big as the whole house. You charge him. It's like running into the side of the living room wall.

So you back up to get a running start. You rush at him again. He falls down with a snarl and rolls on the carpet. You leap on him with a shout. He lifts you up like a toy. Your stomach flutters as you ride the wave of air.

He flings you down on the other side, helping you land with his arms. It hurts just a little, and you are breathing hard. You fight the urge to whimper, but instead you put on your fiercest look. As you jump up, he crouches, smiles, and beckons you with his hand.

"Come on," he growls. "Let's see what you are made of."

With your best scowl on your face, you charge again. He pushes back. So do you. You rebound, bounce off the sofa, and come at him once again. You grunt. He grunts. Your mom leaves the room, shaking her head.

Your little arms seem tiny next to his biceps, but your thin muscles are straining harder than you knew you could. As you both shove against each other, it feels like a standoff. You push against him; nothing moves.

You can't believe it. His arms give just a little bit. You're winning. You have almost run out of energy, but you dig down deep in your heart and you push even harder. He pushes back, but then he gives a little more, just a little bit. You roar.

Somehow you are on top of him, driving both his arms down slowly with more muscle power than you knew you had. Your arms ache, but you keep on going. You can't stop now. Both of you are groaning with the effort. Leaning with all your weight, you push and you push and you push. His arms move slightly under your pressure, getting slowly closer, slowly closer to the floor.

His arms hit the carpet. You've done it. You can't believe it. You have actually pinned your own dad.

Part 1

Relentless

God is educating you; that's why you must never drop out. He's treating you as dear children. This trouble you're in isn't punishment; it's training, the normal experience of children.

—Hebrews 12:7 *The Message*

Endure hardship as discipline; God is treating you as his children. For what children are not disciplined by their father?

—Hebrews 12:7 NIV

Chapter 1

Grit

Jacob (Genesis 32—33)

And Jacob was left alone. And a man wrestled with him until the breaking of the day. When the man saw that he did not prevail against Jacob, he touched his hip socket, and Jacob's hip was put out of joint as he wrestled with him. Then he said, "Let me go, for the day has broken." But Jacob said, "I will not let you go unless you bless me." And he said to him, "What is your name?" And he said, "Jacob." Then he said, *"Your name shall no longer be called Jacob, but Israel, for you have striven with God and with men, and have prevailed."* Then Jacob asked him, "Please tell me your name." But he said, "Why is it that you ask my name?" And there he blessed him. So Jacob called the name of the place Peniel, saying, "For I have seen God face to face, and yet my life has been delivered." The sun rose upon him as he passed Penuel, limping because of his hip.

—Genesis 32:24–31

Every movement of a branch sounds like an intruder. The night seems to last forever. You can't sleep. You have no idea what will happen tomorrow. Some of the possibilities would lead to the loss of everything. The clean sting of the blade across the front of your neck. The draining away of your own life there in the midday heat. Maybe the murder of your own children before you die, their frightened eyes looking to you for protection. You had to get alone before the morning.

Another crack of a branch. That couldn't be the wind. No one knows you are here. It's nothing. You stop breathing, trying to listen. Even the insects get quiet. Silence. It's nothing. When will the dawn come?

Then he is on you. Out of nowhere he jumps on your back and wraps his arm around your neck. You can't breathe. You reach for your sword, but he drags you across the ground away from it like you are a bag of wheat. He pushes your head forward, and you are about to black out. This is the end. You think of your wives, your children, your many goats, your many sheep.

You pull on the stranger's arm with every fiber of your strength. His arm gives a little. You can breathe again. Just barely. He hasn't won yet. You twist your body and push hard, flinging him over your back. He hits the dirt with a grunt. You roll on the ground as he clings to you. The gravel presses against your back and your head. It doesn't matter.

You're not winning, but neither is he. Every time you think he is going to strangle you, you twist his fingers enough so that you can breathe. It is too dark to see his face, but he seems very strong—maybe a great hunter or a warrior. Is this your brother Esau? No. He keeps you just far enough away from your own sword. You can smell his breath, his sweat. He touches your hip. It hurts like crazy. But he hasn't won yet.

The night creeps on like a wounded dog. You feel as though you are fighting yourself, the darkness, your fears, a wave, some large animal, your own brother. You are losing your bearings.

You hear a voice inside of you. "You will die tonight. Esau will win. None of the promises of God for you are true. Give up."

You shake your head. Something rises in you, a deep growl in your chest. He's not going to win. Not after all this.

The fight is unthinkable. It goes on beyond imagining; it's endless. Neither you nor he can pull off a victory. Where is the dawn? Finally, out of the corner of your eye, you see a thin rim of light along the horizon. You hear a bird sing a solitary note. Then another note.

"Let me go," he speaks huskily.

No way. This is not a normal fight. You sense the strange otherness about him, the power of the night before the dawn, something quiet like the stars and yet massive like a black storm. Why not? You go for it; you don't know why. You grip him even more tightly—you are relentless.

"I won't let you go until you bless me," you hiss between your teeth. You surprise even yourself. What are you thinking? You grip his arms in yours with a new ferocity.

He is breathing hard, but his voice is now calm. "What is your name?" He asks. The bird stops singing.

"What is your name?" he asks. What a thing to ask after a fight. You are the one who should be asking questions, not the loser.

Your name—that is like asking what your nature is. What you are known for. Who are you? You think about your brother, about your many goats and sheep, about your old, blind, gullible father, about your mother, about your uncle who cheated you again and again and whom you also thwarted. Then you think once more about the many goats and sheep you have acquired.

You wait a long time before you answer, but you hold his arms tight. You think about that name you were given so long ago and the reason for it. Yes. You know what the name Jacob implies. From the very beginning you were an overreacher, a supplanter, even a cheater. That's who you are. You say that name, hoarsely whispering the word, knowing its meaning. "Cheater," you speak slowly. "That is my name. Cheater."

Another bird begins to sing in the dark. But maybe it is not quite as dark as it was. You can even see the outline of his face, severe beyond words. But you can't make out his expression.

5

His voice is firm. "You shall no longer be called 'Cheater.' Now you will be called 'One Who Struggles with God.' You have wrestled with God and with people, and you have won."

You have won. It's hard to believe. You release him, and he slips away in the dark like a huge black cat. You sit on the ground, in the rocks, for a long time. Now you can see the spare outline of the scrubby trees and the bushes. You look at the red imprint of the gravel on the back of your hands and on your knees. More birds begin to sing as the dawn arrives.

You stand to pick up your clothes. You find you can't walk without limping; it hurts so much. You head toward your brother, the one you have been fighting with and running from all your life. This is the day.

For some reason you think about your grandfather, Abraham, and the stories he told.

Chapter 2

Gall

Abraham (Genesis 18)

So the men turned from there and went toward Sodom, but Abraham still stood before the Lord. Then Abraham drew near and said, "Will you indeed sweep away the righteous with the wicked? Suppose there are fifty righteous within the city. Will you then sweep away the place and not spare it for the fifty righteous who are in it? Far be it from you to do such a thing, to put the righteous to death with the wicked, so that the righteous fare as the wicked! Far be that from you! Shall not the Judge of all the earth do what is just?" And the Lord said, "If I find at Sodom fifty righteous in the city, I will spare the whole place for their sake."

Abraham answered and said, "Behold, I have undertaken to speak to the Lord, I who am but dust and ashes. Suppose five of the fifty righteous are lacking. Will you destroy the whole city for lack of five?" And he said, "I will not destroy it if I find forty-five there." Again he spoke to him and said, "Suppose forty are found there." He answered, "For the sake of forty I will not do it." Then he said, "Oh let not the Lord be angry, and I will speak. Suppose thirty are found there." He answered, "I will not do it, if I find thirty there." He said, "Behold, I have undertaken to speak to the Lord. Suppose twenty are found there." He answered, "For the sake of twenty I will not destroy it." *Then he said, "Oh let not the Lord be angry, and I will speak again but this once. Suppose ten are found there." He answered, "For the sake of ten I will not destroy it."* And the Lord went his way, when

he had finished speaking to Abraham, and Abraham returned
to his place.

—Genesis 18:22–33

Your descendants won't ever understand. The waiting. The struggles. More waiting. The dreariness. The failures. More waiting. This visitation.

You look up and see them one day at noon. Tall visitors. The heat from the sand makes their bodies wave and shimmer as though they aren't even walking on the ground.

Three of them. You hurry to be the proper host—bread and meat and milk. Their faces are, well, different—very stern, very generous. It seems right that not many words are spoken. After the meal they give a bless-ing—an astonishing, ridicuous, preposterous promise. But it places within you a tiny sliver of hope.

Sarah will have a son. You are way too old now. Sarah is also way too old. More than way too old.

Sarah was listening. She laughs out loud at the promise. The laughter is awkward, inappropriate. Like chuckling during a sacrifice. The visitors' looks are disconcerting. Her denial of the whole thing makes matters even worse. The hesitant conversation is an embarrassment.

This is a visitation. The intense temperature in the middle of the day creates a feeling of oddness. You sense the rare quality of the moment. The hair on your arms stands on end, even in the heat. Will your family accept this story, this promise? No one else would. You watch as two of the visitors walk away across the desert, toward Sodom, their bodies once again waving in the heat as they grow smaller.

It's not going to be good. You know judgment is coming, that somehow the Lord himself is here in all this. In a flash deep in your chest, you see the violence in the two cities in the distance, the hurt, the destructive contagious selfishness that will eventually infect the entire region. And in time's river it will poison many generations beyond your comprehension. This is God's severe word upon them, his kindness to the future.

Or is it? In a way God Himself visited you. Can't you talk to Him? So what if it is inappropriate to object here in this weighty moment? Your own nephew lives over there. Maybe there are other good people in those cities. It doesn't seem fair. Can you say anything?

You do it. You speak up—to the Judge of the entire world no less. You can't believe you are doing it, but it just doesn't seem right.

You go ahead and challenge His justice. "What if there are fifty good people in the town?" You sound as though you are bargaining for fruit in the market. "Surely You wouldn't slay the good people with the wicked, would You?" You hope you are not appearing to be lecturing. Your voice almost cracks, and you sound a bit like you are bleating.

Never have you spoken this way before, even to an earthly authority. You've been trained to know how to get by, always to be the guest on other peoples' land, always deferring to the host. Remember who you are talking to. This is God. You wait to be annihilated, like a drop of water thrown into the fire. It could happen just like that.

A long silence follows. You are not sure if the silence means fury or something else.

Finally the answer. "If there are fifty good people, righteous people, I will spare the whole place."

Now you know the boundaries are not rigid. You can't help yourself. You press on. You are obsequious but persistent, certain that you are hugely irritating to the Lord of the universe. You draw on your petty power to reason.

"Suppose five of the fifty people are lacking. Maybe they have gone on a journey. Will You still destroy the place because five righteous people are lacking?" This is the kind of classic bargaining you use when you are buying a goat. You know how small it sounds.

"I will not destroy the city if there are forty-five."

"What about forty?" You almost stop yourself, but plunge ahead.

"No. Then I won't destroy it."

"Don't be angry with me. What about thirty?"

"I won't do it if there are thirty."

How far can you push? You don't know. What's the outer border to your own cheekiness? It's a risk. You sense you may be getting to the limit of benevolence, the limit of mercy when too much mercy will hurt so many. "What about twenty?"

"I won't do it then."

You think about your nephew and his family. Silly in their own way, a bit self-centered, shallow, all of them, but you think of how Lot followed you as you stepped out to follow God. He didn't know what he was doing.

A ripple of fear passes through you. The Lord, your Creator, He gave you any sense of justice you have. Now are you going to use your feeble sense of fairness, throw it in His face, and try to talk God out of His own vast majestic sense of right?

Yes you are.

"This is the last time I will speak, I promise. What if there are ten innocent people there in the city?" You felt again, like a blast of heat, the cruelty of those city-dwellers, their brutality, their petty justifications of all the things that destroy so many.

You sense that somehow you have pushed too far, that you are talking to the Ruler over heaven and earth, and you increasingly sound like you are instructing *Him* on justice, of all things. The silence that follows your request is excruciating. The other two men are wavy specks in the distance now.

"For the sake of ten I will not destroy it."

You perceive something like a twinkle in His eye. You feel a sense of doubt. Were you pushing Him, or was He pushing you?

For a moment you think about all the promises you have been given, and you haven't seen any practical evidence of any of it—none at all. Descendants like the stars of the sky. *No.* A huge swath of land that will keep you from always being a wanderer, a nomad. *No.* Offspring that are princes and princesses . . . *no.*

No, no, no. No, but you may yet have that child . . .

Chapter 3

Doggedness

Isaac (Genesis 26)

So he built an altar there and called upon the name of the L<small>ORD</small> and pitched his tent there. And there Isaac's servants dug a well. When Abimelech went to him from Gerar with Ahuzzath his adviser and Phicol the commander of his army, *Isaac said to them, "Why have you come to me, seeing that you hate me and have sent me away from you?"* They said, "We see plainly that the L<small>ORD</small> has been with you. So we said, let there be a sworn pact between us, between you and us, and let us make a covenant with you, that you will do us no harm, just as we have not touched you and have done to you nothing but good and have sent you away in peace. You are now the blessed of the L<small>ORD</small>." So he made them a feast, and they ate and drank. In the morning they rose early and exchanged oaths. And Isaac sent them on their way, and they departed from him in peace.

—Genesis 26:25–31

You are Abraham's famous child. Everyone talked about your birth. So what? What about all those promises God gave your father?

The dead carcass of a scrawny goat by the side of the road. Nothing but bones and a hardened hide. The clumps of dry grass on the plain with big patches of dirt in between. The hunger on the face of the old woman, begging—the tendons on her neck as distinct as ropes. Famine. This is some blessing. You hate it. But . . . you refuse to leave.

Not that you didn't want to leave. Everyone else said you should go to Egypt where the great river provides the moisture you are so desperate for—desperate for your flocks and, in the end, for your own family.

But God told you to stay, so you stayed. He spoke to you, just as He spoke to your dad. Yet you didn't really even do the staying in the right way. You got scared. Things got fuzzy. Easy for someone else to judge afterwards. You saw the looks in the men's eyes when they saw your wife Rebecca.

You are an outsider. You couldn't put it into words, but you knew deep down as you saw their faces. Survival—staying alive in a hostile land. So you told them Rebecca was your sister, just like your dad had done with your mom Sarah so many years before. You pretended to yourself that it wasn't a lie. That whole thing didn't work out so well, did it?

But you kept on. You didn't leave. Some of your own family grumbled, called you bullheaded for not going to Egypt like the rest of the smarter herdsmen. You even took the time to plant in a season of drought. In the middle of the famine you got an abundant crop. An incredible crop. Go figure. You felt God's goodness as you walked through the waves of golden grain. Your family got quiet.

Now the crop brings you new problems. Once again you saw it in their eyes as you came to the market to sell the abundance in the midst of a famine. The looks of the people there but no words. This isn't good, but you persist. Your family whispers in the tent again. You should leave. Go to Egypt. It's safer.

These people don't like you, and they didn't like your dad. They filled up your father's wells out of sheer meanness. The smallness of it all. If you start thinking about it, your mouth starts tasting bitter and dry. So you refuse to think about it. If God is supposed to be blessing you, the son of

Abraham—why is He making it so hard? What possible reason is there? Why do you feel so pressed?

Yet here you are. It was still a surprise, at least a little bit. The king calls you in. He fumbles for a while, but finally he tells you to leave. Why? You know why. But you are not running to Egypt. Certainly not now.

Instead you go into the adjacent valley. You go to the wells of your father, the ones that were ruined. You start to dig again—spade work, in the heat of the day, pile of dirt after pile of dirt. Recovering wells that were ruined.

After all that digging, you even find a well with running water. The water tasted so sweet in the heat of the day after all that work. How strange life is—good fortune mixed with hard fortune. It always seems to be that way.

Another challenge. You should have expected it. Still it hurts. Your herdsmen are furious, indignant—telling you that the herdsman of the area say the water is theirs. But you won't leave. You just dig another well in another place. Spade work again—pile of dirt after pile of dirt in the heat of the day. Then the same herdsmen insist on the incredible— this new well is theirs too. They make a case for it. They don't see the unfairness of what they are doing. Your family is in an uproar, feeding on the delicacies of obvious injustice.

You refuse to whine about it anymore. And then, well, you just dig another well. Shovelful after shovelful. You pretend you don't hear the grumbling of your own people, your own family. You hear the phrase "pig headed" again behind your back. Why don't you just relent and leave? You've dug four, five, six wells or more now, blessing the whole area. No one from outside bothers you this time—at least for a while.

But one day at noon you see the king and his two most trusted advisors approaching—looking a bit awkward, just like the last time you saw them. You brace yourself for the order to leave once again.

"Why do you come to me, since you hate me and sent me away?" You want to be courteous, but you have to be honest. You notice how shrill your own voice sounds.

They look at the ground and search for words. They talk about other things, the weather, the goats. Finally they come out with it—they tell you that they see how you keep prospering in the middle of the famine. Your family listens inside the tent.

Of all things—they want to make an agreement of peace with you. You are silent, stunned. This is your chance to turn the tables on them. This is the time to humiliate them for the multiple times you had to start again, to dig again, to move again, for the disrespect of it all, and for their disregard. You feel the surge of justifiable vengeance rise in your throat. It will be easy to rub their poverty into their own faces.

But you refuse. Your father Abraham said that you would bless all people. Well here is a small start, not what you expected. Your family may call it bull-headedness. But you make an agreement, and there, as the famine is still raging, you make an abundant feast for them, for the king and his men. Their faces look puzzled now. But they eat—a lot.

You are not a talker. You can't really put it into words. You are not the kind of pioneer your father Abraham was. But there's a stubbornness about winning, and then there's a kind of stubbornness about allowing yourself to "lose." You heard what your dad did with his nephew. Your dad let him have the best land, even though as the uncle he should have been the one to choose. You saw how your dad sometimes had his own way of persisting in losing, even though somehow in the end it wasn't losing. You just can't put it into words.

You will never be able to say what it felt like that day your father took you to the mountain and prepared to cut your throat—never. Other people can do the talking. But somehow you know that there is a time to be relentless, and there is a time to relent. There is a time to fight, and there is a time when you let yourself lose for something more important. In both choices you have to be steadfast.

Your dad did that. In his own way he was steadfast in believing. And he said that someday your people will be princes . . .

Chapter 4

Stamina

Hagar (Genesis 21)

So Abraham rose early in the morning and took bread and a skin of water and gave it to Hagar, putting it on her shoulder, along with the child, and sent her away. And she departed and wandered in the wilderness of Beersheba. When the water in the skin was gone, she put the child under one of the bushes. *Then she went and sat down opposite him a good way off, about the distance of a bowshot, for she said, "Let me not look on the death of the child."* And as she sat opposite him, she lifted up her voice and wept. And God heard the voice of the boy, and the angel of God called to Hagar from heaven and said to her, "What troubles you, Hagar? Fear not, for God has heard the voice of the boy where he is. Up! Lift up the boy, and hold him fast with your hand, for I will make him into a great nation." Then God opened her eyes, and she saw a well of water. And she went and filled the skin with water and gave the boy a drink. And God was with the boy, and he grew up. He lived in the wilderness and became an expert with the bow.

—Genesis 21:14–20

Isaac is no hero to you. In fact just the birth of Isaac changed everything for you. You don't feel like a princess, and your son Ishmael is no prince. You've given up. This is the end of the road. You and your boy will die out here in the desert with no food and no water. You don't even know exactly where you are any more. The brutal sun is burning right above you. There is no shade—just a few scrubby bushes.

This is the limit of endurance. You are feeling dizzy, and your mouth is dry. You are not sure you are even thinking straight anymore. Ishmael has stopped complaining. He is quiet and listless now as you carry him. Step by step, mile after mile.

All because of Isaac. He is just a baby, but everything is now different. So what if your son Ishmael laughed at their ceremony? Ishmael's just a boy. The laughter was like dropping a torch on a pile of dry grass. Sarah, your mistress, was furious. After so long she finally had her child. A lot of talk in the tent ensued, talk that you didn't get to hear.

All you know is that Abraham, the father of your own child, woke you up early in the morning, gave you some bread and water, and sent you away. You were in shock. Abraham said very little, and you didn't either. He was still standing there, watching, even when you had walked a long way away, Ishmael holding your hand. Ishmael was quiet too as the sun rose before you.

Now the bread and the water are gone. They have been gone a long time. Your will to continue is also gone. What's the use? You have no family anymore. You have no place to go. No money. No one to help you. Your Ishmael is just a boy.

You've always been an outsider, just like you are now. Not quite good enough with Abraham and Sarah. You ran away before, and now you have been sent away. Your head aches. You slowly realize this is the way you are going to die. Precious Ishmael. You put him down under a little bush, a tiny spot of shade in all the scorching heat. There is an endpoint to what you can do. You leave him there and walk on. No one will know. You can't just watch him die.

You walk on farther and collapse in the dirt. There isn't even a bush to lie under. For the first time since you left Abraham, you weep. A wailing rises up from your chest. The looks, the orders, the exclusion, the ejection, the hopelessness of it all as you prepare to die.

Then you hear the voice again. The voice that has helped you in the past, calm and firm. The voice says to get up and go get your son. He will live and be great.

Then you see it. It must have always been there and you hadn't seen it—right under your nose. A well there in the distance. Water. Life.

Your son will have no father present in his life. You have no resources. You don't know where you are going next. So what? Why did God push you in this desert? Why didn't He give you water when you first ran out? For that matter, why didn't God give Sarah a child decades ago so you wouldn't be in this mess in the first place?

Once you start, the why questions go on and on. And right now—why did you get pushed to the limit of your endurance before God gave you a way out? You thought of this many times as you watched your boy grow up. Isaac's offspring will be princes. Well so will the offspring of your Ishmael.

Chapter 5

Nerve

Moses (Numbers 13—14)

And the L̲ord̲ said to Moses, "How long will this people despise me? And how long will they not believe in me, in spite of all the signs that I have done among them? I will strike them with the pestilence and disinherit them, and I will make of you a nation greater and mightier than they." But Moses said to the Lord, "Then the Egyptians will hear of it, for you brought up this people in your might from among them, and they will tell the inhabitants of this land. They have heard that you, O Lord, are in the midst of this people. For you, O Lord, are seen face to face, and your cloud stands over them and you go before them, in a pillar of cloud by day and in a pillar of fire by night. Now if you kill this people as one man, then the nations who have heard your fame will say, 'It is because the Lord was not able to bring this people into the land that he swore to give to them that he has killed them in the wilderness.' And now, please let the power of the Lord be great as you have promised, saying, 'The Lord is slow to anger and abounding in steadfast love, forgiving iniquity and transgression, but he will by no means clear the guilty, visiting the iniquity of the fathers on the children, to the third and the fourth generation.' *Please pardon the iniquity of this people, according to the greatness of your steadfast love, just as you have forgiven this people, from Egypt until now."* Then the Lord *said, "I have pardoned, according to your word."*

—Numbers 14:11–20

Abraham, Isaac, and Jacob were all told their offspring would be princes. You know the stories about Sarah and about Hagar. What a joke, those promises. You certainly don't feel like a prince. You're furious.

Yes, once you were a prince, and, yes, you murdered a man, all in a stupid blowup. You are not the same man as you were then, but you feel that same rage right now—a bitter fluid in the throat.

This is worse than the whole Aaron-and-golden-calf fiasco. You are actually on the border of the Promised Land, the land flowing with milk and honey, the place you have talked about and dreamed of for so long. But the people have given up once again. Don't they remember? The God of generous Abraham and of persistent Isaac and of conniving Jacob. Those ones had some heart and some pluck. They were relentless. You know the stories, told to you over and over by your mother so long ago.

So your spies saw some "big" people there. Called them giants. Refused to go back, the chickens. The lily-livered, weak, spineless chickens. After all He has done for us. Only Caleb and Joshua had some guts, some backbone.

"We can do this!" Caleb and Jacob said. The rest of the people whimpered and blithered and blamed you. They want another leader. It isn't their fault, they say. They just want to go back to Egypt—yes, to slavery and whips and forced labor and endless weariness. You see it plainly—Pharaoh is dead, but he is still, even now, living inside of them. He controls their minds even now. You can't hide your fury. The crowd gets ugly, and it looks like they may even kill Joshua and Caleb. Unbelievable. Things aren't turning out the way you planned.

Then something happens. The Presence comes, God's glory—heavy, severe. It's here. It's tangible and yet can't be touched. It is right here and yet has no boundaries. Everything changes for you.

You don't know what the people can hear. It doesn't matter. But you also realize that you yourself don't know what real anger is. This is like nothing you've seen from the Presence before. It is this white-hot intensity that makes your trifling vexation look weak and puny. Your own ire is rapidly draining away in the presence of this earthquake of passion. This fire is the intensity of a lover who has found out he has been betrayed. It is the intensity of a mother that, in her insane love, threatens to kill her own cubs, she is so incensed by their self-destructive stupidity.

You know when not to say anything.

God, the God of Abraham and Jacob, says He will disinherit them, strike them down. He will instead make *you* into a great nation.

You are stunned. What is He doing? Is He serious in His divine purpose? Is He appealing to your desire to be a real prince once again, remembered and admired for all time as the father of God's people? Forget Abraham. Think of it. You would be portrayed by God, no less, as the one who stepped in and cleaned up the mess as a result of these whining and spineless people. You can see it in your heart, generation after generation telling your story—the great *Father* Moses. God said it. It must be right.

But then you remember. The voice of your mother. Those whispered stories of struggle when you were still a child in the palace of luxury. Your people. The hue of your skin. The shape of your nose. That one spindly little Hebrew girl in the sun with her thin wrists, forced to make bricks with no lunch. Your own anger and your own crime. Your flight. The plagues. The battles in the heat, your tribe, your family. Your people.

You won't let Him go through with it.

You marshal up your strength to actually disagree with the Almighty, this hurricane of purpose. What can you really say? He navigated your education in Egypt and in the desert. He made your heart, your mind, your fumbling tongue, your sense of justice, your care for your people. And besides, if you speak, you might even get burned by the intensity of His determination, a determination ready to flare up at any flicker of resistance.

You press on anyway. You feel foolish as you marshal up your little arguments to "win over" God. What will the Egyptians say? People will think God isn't able to deliver His people. Even you feel the childishness of these arguments. He knows you. He knows you are trying to placate Him, to calm Him down. Besides, you say—remember, God is merciful and gracious, *slow to anger*, abounding in steadfast love. You throw His own words back at Him. At God Himself. You can't stop. These faithless, deceitful, complaining, stupid, childish people—they are God's people, but they are your people too, and you will fight for them, even if it kills you. And it might.

You wait to be annihilated by the fierce presence.

But then, after a heavy silence, God relents. He gives in. What is going on? You have won an argument with God. You win. He doesn't destroy the people; He pardons them. With conditions. The conditions are fair enough, all things considered. And they give hope, hope for the Promised Land, the land free of slavery, the land of plenty, the land where you and your people will no longer be wanderers like Abraham, no longer the awkward guests of others anymore.

Someday things will be different. Your people will all be rulers and princes, not slaves ever again. You will make it to that land that was pledged.

Chapter 6

Courage

Joshua (Joshua 5)

> When Joshua was by Jericho, he lifted up his eyes and looked, and behold, a man was standing before him with his drawn sword in his hand. And Joshua went to him and said to him, *"Are you for us, or for our adversaries?" And he said, "No; but I am the commander of the army of the* Lord*. Now I have come."* And Joshua fell on his face to the earth and worshiped and said to him, "What does my lord say to his servant?" And the commander of the Lord's army said to Joshua, "Take off your sandals from your feet, for the place where you are standing is holy." And Joshua did so.
>
> —Joshua 5:13–15

Moses didn't make it to the new land he talked about for so many years. It's hard to believe he's really dead. Moses was your mentor and always made the final decisions. Now it is up to you. Mighty Jericho and its walls. God keeps telling you to have courage.

Even so, you are still scared. You walk outside the city of Jericho, needing some time away from the others, thinking about the attack. The fortifications look so strong. More than strong—*impregnable* would be a better word. Able to withstand many invaders. A siege won't work. They have plenty of resources and supplies within those massive city walls.

It's all so different. You are all alone here on the ridge. Moses was always so much older, and he always had more experience than you. Sure he was a little severe, and sure he had his faults. But you always knew where you stood. You and Moses had experienced both victory and defeat together. What would he do now? At least in wilderness, you learned how to survive. This is all so different.

What is that up ahead? A huge man, a warrior, just standing there. He doesn't come to parlay. His sword, a massive sword, is drawn. The look on his face is austere.

Should you retreat and get more help? What if all of Jericho is filled with warriors like this man? In some ways he is your worst nightmare. And his hands aren't open toward you. His sword is drawn. He doesn't come as a friend. This is going to be a fight.

Oh well. What can you do? You can't just walk away. You are too far away to call for assistance. You breathe in and then take a step toward him, your hand on your own sword. You take another step. Even the insects are quiet. Your hand twitches.

Your voice sounds reedy. You try to make it sound stronger. Come on— you have fought many battles with Moses as your leader. Now you have to do it all alone.

"Are you for us, or for our enemies?" you find yourself asking. This seems like a clear request. Are you a friend or an enemy?

You are closer now. You notice the slight sparkle in his eye, even the faintest upturning of his mouth—a strange expression since he is so serious.

"No," he says.

What does that mean? No is not an answer to your question. In your mind, it is either one or the other—either for the Hebrews or for the Canaanites. Friend or foe. He is either an ally or an opponent. Is he testing you, somehow? It almost feels as though he is being cryptic just to see what you are made of.

"I have now come as the commander of the army of the Lord."

Commander? The commander? You see it now. It's true.

He could have sliced through your weapons in an instant as you marched toward him with your hand on your sword, demanding an answer. But he didn't. Of course he made it clear he wasn't on your side either. It doesn't work like that. There must be other answers to your puny little question about whose side he is on.

Jericho before you. Does each generation have to learn what courage is over and over again? Can't you just inherit it from those who were strong before you? Can't you just receive it from someone else like receiving a loaf of bread—without all this exertion? This is like when you were with Moses, and yet it is different too. You sense you are being pressed to see how you respond. So this is what it feels like, this holy ground. You take off your shoes. You have no other options.

Chapter 7

Loyalty

Ruth (Ruth 1)

"Turn back, my daughters; go your way, for I am too old to have a husband. If I should say I have hope, even if I should have a husband this night and should bear sons, would you therefore wait till they were grown? Would you therefore refrain from marrying? No, my daughters, for it is exceedingly bitter to me for your sake that the hand of the Lord has gone out against me." Then they lifted up their voices and wept again. And Orpah kissed her mother-in-law, but Ruth clung to her. And she said, "See, your sister-in-law has gone back to her people and to her gods; return after your sister-in-law." But Ruth said, "Do not urge me to leave you or to return from following you. For where you go I will go, and where you lodge I will lodge. Your people shall be my people, and your God my God. Where you die I will die, and there will I be buried. May the Lord do so to me and more also if anything but death parts me from you." *And when Naomi saw that she was determined to go with her, she said no more.*

—Ruth 1:12–18

You heard about Joshua from your mother-in-law, but you're no warrior. And that was so long ago. Right now you don't have a lot of options at all. Your husband is dead. Your sister-in-law's husband is dead. Your mother-in-law's husband is dead. These men would be the ones to provide protection and resources. Your mother-in-law is going home, to a place where you would be considered not only a foreigner but sometimes a hated foreigner. So your only real option is to stay in your own country and find another husband. In fact that is what your sister-in-law plans to do.

You hate being so dependent. You hate scrambling for some way to just have some food for the day. You are a woman. You are a widow. You are almost on the bottom rung of the ladder in your tribe.

But you look at your mother-in-law Naomi. She's got fewer choices than you do. She's old, and she understands the situation. She has already given you an honorable way to leave her. Your sister-in-law Orpah knows she is right and has already made her decision.

And what about you? Do you really have more than one option? Probably not, if you want a husband. Naomi's people are famous for being selective about intermarrying. You will have very few alternatives if you go with her.

Steadfast love. Naomi has talked about that. Naomi's God is the God of steadfast love. Merciful and gracious, abounding in steadfast love. Naomi has suffered so much—so many disappointments. She is honest about her own bitterness in life. Still, what about you?

You decide to pass on that bitterness part. You're no warrior, but you can be steadfast too. Just like Naomi's God. You make the choice. Orpah kisses your mother-in-law and walks away sadly.

You hold Naomi in your arms as you both watch Orpah walk way. A younger woman holding an older woman. Naomi has told you about Abraham. Abraham gave up the better choice for his own nephew though Abraham deserved to get the better land and with it the better opportunities. You can give up the better choice too.

You don't say any of that. You simply say you will go where she goes; you will live where she lives. Her God will be your God. Your sister-in-law will probably find a husband soon and start life again. Maybe a husband with resources—many goats and sheep and grain and workers. She's still attractive and strong. You could have done that too, in your own country. As you walk you feel the loss of all the obvious solutions, a loss deep within your stomach. You hold Naomi's arm as you proceed, two unprotected women on a road full of dangers.

Steadfast. Your care for her is more important. You will both find a way, for good or for ill. The choice you have made has real consequences. You will probably die without a husband, without children, and among a people that often consider you an enemy. With no descendants, no one will remember you even a few years after you are gone.

No matter. You take another step on the road. Your feet feel so heavy, but you grit your teeth and keep going. Eventually you start looking for a safe place to sleep for the night.

Chapter 8

Faithfulness

Hannah (1 Samuel 1)

As she continued praying before the LORD, Eli observed her mouth. Hannah was speaking in her heart; only her lips moved, and her voice was not heard. Therefore Eli took her to be a drunken woman. And Eli said to her, *"How long will you go on being drunk? Put your wine away from you."* But Hannah answered, *"No, my lord, I am a woman troubled in spirit. I have drunk neither wine nor strong drink, but I have been pouring out my soul before the LORD.* Do not regard your servant as a worthless woman, for all along I have been speaking out of my great anxiety and vexation." Then Eli answered, "Go in peace, and the God of Israel grant your petition that you have made to him." And she said, "Let your servant find favor in your eyes." Then the woman went her way and ate, and her face was no longer sad.

—1 Samuel 1:12–18

Descendants won't come for you either. No one will remember you. And here's the last straw. Year after year you pray the same thing—a child, one child. That's all. Now you come, as you do each year, to pray for a child, and the priest, no less, totally misunderstands you.

Blended families are tough, and your husband's other wife has children so easily. No problem for her. And she provokes you, makes catty remarks, and rolls her eyes with the neighbors. With her words, she pokes her finger into that tender throbbing wound in your heart whenever she can. It gives her great pleasure.

And it doesn't take much to provoke you anyway. This is the one aching hollowness of your life—no children. Nothing else matters to you.

Your husband doesn't help with his ham-fisted attempts to mollify you. Giving you an extra portion of food at worship only makes you feel worse. It just points out the problem and makes you the object of pity to others. You don't want to look pathetic. His words are his attempt to encourage—"Aren't I worth more than ten sons?" Just not the right thing to say—you can't explain it to him through the tears. He doesn't get it.

You keep going on, year after year, but you wake up in the middle of the night, weeping. Your husband just snores. Still you don't give up. You keep praying and praying. You've heard the stories of Sarah, how she waited so long before her son Isaac was born. More importantly you've heard the stories of Jacob—"I won't let You go unless You bless me!" That's it.

So here you are again—at worship at Shiloh once again, praying with a shredded heart once again, too tender for anyone to heal, once again. You haven't eaten it hurts so much—your appetite is completely gone. People tell you how thin and gaunt you have become. So be it. They don't understand.

The tears come. You pray fervently, mouthing the words strongly but not making noise, not disturbing others. If you get a son you will give him completely over to the Lord. You release your child for God. You keep praying. You won't let God go until He blesses you.

And Eli the priest sees you all alone, rocking and weeping and mouthing the words in great intensity, and he doesn't understand either. He thinks you are drunk. Alcoholism is such a problem in the community. Here you are—you are doing your best, and even this holy priest completely misunderstands your heart and your motives.

What an insult. A wave of discouragement passes over you like warm muddy water. It's time to leave the priest, the worship—it's time to leave God. Why not just march out and give up? It's not like you have just prayed a day or two. You have prayed for years and years with no results.

But no. If anything, you are persistent. You don't lash out at Eli the priest. You make the choice to show respect. Even if there is the smallest of chances, you don't want to block any way that God might bless you. What if this awkward moment were a way that God is pressing you, pressing to see if you will revert to easy petulance in the face of disappointment? You don't know why this is so hard, but you don't let go.

You explain to the priest that alcohol isn't involved at all, that you are praying and are as serious as you can be. You know Eli has his own family problems with sons who are flippant and callous. He pauses a moment and really looks at you for the first time.

Wait a minute. Does Eli send you a tiny lifeline of hope? Yes he does. Does he understand what he is saying? You don't know. He simply says to go in peace, that God has granted your request.

Now you have another choice. You can easily disregard what Eli said. You have had so many disappointments through the years. So many people have said words of hope and promise just to make you feel better. Isn't this simply more of the same? It would be so easy to just give up on God.

On the other hand you still have the power to make your own choice. You can receive these words of hope, accept them, dwell in them, mix them with your own faithfulness. You decide to take that course. Past disappointments can either drive you away from God or they can toughen your heart to be even more relentless.

What's the best way to show that things have changed inside of you? You relax and eat a big meal, a double portion. Your husband smiles at you and is happy.

Chapter 9

Toughness

David (Psalm 34)

(Of David, when he changed his behavior before Abimelech, so that he drove him out, and he went away.)

I will bless the LORD at all times; his praise shall continually be in my mouth. My soul makes its boast in the LORD; let the humble hear and be glad. Oh, magnify the LORD with me, and let us exalt his name together! I sought the Lord, and he answered me and delivered me from all my fears. Those who look to him are radiant, and their faces shall never be ashamed. This poor man cried, and the LORD heard him and saved him out of all his troubles.

—Psalm 34:1–6

You know the whole story about how Samuel was born, and you even knew his mother Hannah before she died. You've heard the stories of your own great-grandmother, who has also already passed on. Her name was Ruth. Did your great-grandmother ever have times when she didn't know what to do?

You also know the stories of the warriors from way back in the past—especially Joshua with all his victories in the Promised Land. You've heard them all your life. Joshua probably never felt afraid. If only you had Joshua's kind of courage. And for a while, when you were younger, you thought you did. You even thought you were going to be a ruler here. Why else did Samuel anoint you so long ago, bringing you in from the fields, making a big deal over you in front of your brothers and your father? Things went pretty well for a while, you giant killer.

Giant killer. Strange how it happens in life, when things go sour. Defeats often seem to come from the victories. The king didn't want you to be king, despite your deep faith in God and God's desire for good for you. And what about your best friend, the man who should be next in line to be king? It's all so complicated. Now other people who were innocent have been killed because of you. You, the famous young warrior, who always wrote songs about how God was on your side, had to run like a scared lamb.

Well it looks like God lost. You even ran to your people's enemies for safety. That didn't work out so well either. Just to live, you, the great warrior, had to pretend, to lie. You had to act like you were crazy, spit dribbling down your beard. Yes, you got away—but not like a warrior.

Now you are in a cave, not a palace. What happened to God's promise? All your support is gone. Your king hates you, your best friend can't be with you, your family is in danger because of you, and you are separated from all your people. You are certainly not living like a king.

The world seems pretty bleak looking out from the mouth of this dank cave. And boring. Everything is silent, dry, vacant. Ready to give up? You and the God you sing about so much have failed. Nothing has gone according to plan. You started out with that big victory, but you are finishing weak, very weak. Maybe this is always the way it goes.

So what kind of song will you compose now? Go ahead. A song of defeat and despair—your final song for a faith that failed. It hasn't been fair. You gave it your all for a while. Time to move on to something else.

No, no, no, no. You refuse.

Just think of it—you are in a cave, but you are alive. You have been humiliated, but you are still breathing, thank God. You remember again the stories you have heard about Joshua, about Jacob, about Abraham,

Sarah, and about Moses. And what about Job? They made mistakes too and could have quit. But they didn't. Not quite.

You have lost your friends and your people, but you are alive. Alive. Sure, you could have been more like a warrior, but at least your enemies didn't surround you and cut you down in a pool of your own blood. They didn't cut your head off and put it on a pole in a wave of laughter. Things could have gone that way. You don't have much—you don't have a palace, but you have this cave.

You are not going out like this. You are not going out with a whimper. Just think. You haven't gone through anything compared to your ancestor Job. You have no boils on your body. Come on, show them all what you are made of.

You begin to sing, to compose a song for this new situation in the cave. How will you start it? The words echo off the cave as you sing your heart out all alone. "I will bless the Lord at all times. His praise shall *continually* be in my mouth."

Chapter 10

Backbone

Job (Job 38—42)

After the Lord had spoken these words to Job, the Lord said to Eliphaz the Temanite: "My anger burns against you and against your two friends, for you have not spoken of me what is right, as my servant Job has. Now therefore take seven bulls and seven rams and go to my servant Job and offer up a burnt offering for yourselves. And my servant Job shall pray for you, for I will accept his prayer not to deal with you according to your folly. For you have not spoken of me what is right, as my servant Job has." So Eliphaz the Temanite and Bildad the Shuhite and Zophar the Naamathite went and did what the Lord had told them, and the Lord accepted Job's prayer.

—Job 42:7–9

There's no way you are praising the Lord at all times. No way. Not after what has happened. Some people say you have patience. You don't have patience. You have *im*patience.

You couldn't stand the things your friends said to you after the death of your children. It was your fault, they said. You need to repent. Stop being so resistant. Their pious words were insufferable.

In the chaos of your suffering and horror, you cried out, demanded, complained, asked for justice. You even asked for God to be put on trial, insisted you have a hearing.

You wouldn't give up. Your friends couldn't believe your impudence, and as the time went on, despite your sorrow, they became more and more, well, instructive. They could help you. They kept telling you to stop your challenges. But you refused. You asked for—no, demanded—a meeting with the Almighty for a long, long time.

Well God blew all that away. God gave you a meeting. He came in a tornado—that strange dark twisting funnel on the horizon, jumping from place to place, coming toward you, louder and louder. It wasn't what you expected. Instead of comforting you, instead of understanding the pain you had gone through, God told you, straight up, "Put on your big boy pants. Let Me ask you some questions, tough guy."

He totally rearranged your mind. He blew the fuses on all your little challenges. He asked big questions, cosmic questions, questions about the foundation of the world itself, of light, of the springs of the sea. He asked you what you possibly understood about snow and storms and lightning and floods.

And animals. The ones you knew and the ones you didn't know. Ones you had only heard of—strange, wondrous animals. Not one answer came from Him, but His barrage of questions left you with blinking dry eyes and an open, stupid mouth.

Now, so many years later, you still think about it. A lot. You have more wealth, more respect, and more children. Of course, more children will never erase the heartache of the loss of your earlier kids. You are a different person. But you still brood about the encounter with the tornado.

Why did God end the way He did? He was asking questions about animals you had only heard of. Why end with the hippopotamus and the crocodile, or whatever those animals were? They weren't so common where you lived, strange beasts, strong beasts. And how did God praise them?

He said the hippo is immovable. The power of the entire river could rush into his mouth, and he was not frightened. The creature was not even disturbed. Hooks and snares don't even bother him. He's unsinkable.

The crocodile is even tougher, God said. He doesn't speak in soft words or beg for help. Don't even try to stick your spears and harpoons in him. His skin is too hard. Arrows don't bother him. He counts iron as straw. He is one fierce customer.

And that is how God ends His encounter with you. With the image of that hardened super-crocodile—not the wondrous light or the snow or the storms. It's almost as though God is really proud of that flinty creature. His last words to you are about, of all things, the crocodile. His last words, "He is king over all the sons of pride" (Job 41:34).

"Sons of pride." Isn't pride a bad thing? It didn't sound that way when God described it. Why does God end His talk with you on that note—with these two creatures that aren't so pretty to look at but are tough, fierce, unshakeable? What was He trying to tell you?

You think of all your relentless challenges to God, your complaining, your demands that God show up and defend Himself, your refusals to give in to your friends and their over-pious, questionless world. Your friends were horrified at what you said—it was so irreverent and stubborn.

But in the end God says the most puzzling thing of all to your friends. "You have not spoken of me what is right, as my servant Job has" (Job 42:8).

You hadn't spoken to God what was right either. You know that much. God's questions from the whirlwind made you feel as though what you had asked was all wrong. You really didn't know what you were talking about. Why, after all your stupid impudence, was God commending you to your friends? Was it acceptable to ask so many questions and make so many demands? What was God really looking for? After so many years, you think you would know . . .

Chapter 11

Perseverance

Habakkuk (Habakkuk 1—3)

O LORD, how long shall I cry for help, and you will not hear? Or cry to you "Violence!" and you will not save? *Why do you make me see iniquity, and why do you idly look at wrong?* Destruction and violence are before me; strife and contention arise. So the law is paralyzed, and justice never goes forth. For the wicked surround the righteous; so justice goes forth perverted.

—Habakkuk 1:2–4

You want to know too, just like Job, from so long ago. Job asked questions. Why can't you? Something is not right. What is God looking for anyway? The unfairness of it all, the horror. The anger at what is happening to your people, your children. The fact of the matter is, evil people are winning, and your people are losing. It's just not right.

So what do you do? Do you submit to all this and be quiet? No way. The exasperation feels like bile rising up deep inside of you. Who do you go to? Your people? They are completely crushed. The enemy? They are overwhelming.

When to speak and when not to speak. That is what each person has to learn, you suppose. When to ask questions and when not to ask questions. How to pray when your entire world has been destroyed. You go right to God.

The question—how long? How long will prayers go unanswered? You press on, even if it looks as though you are being pushy.

The other question—why? Why are all these troubles to be endured? It is unspeakable what is happening. So you speak. Clear, strong, fierce questions.

God pushes back. He says it's going to get worse. People will sweep over you like the wind. Guilty people. Their own strength is their god.

You quietly listen. This doesn't make sense. Should you just sit submissively and say, "Yes, Lord"? No you will not.

You ask again, and this time you start with the why. Why is God silent when the wicked person swallows up the good person? These evil people let their own tools of destruction become their gods, and then they live in luxury. They think everything is just fine. But everything is not just fine.

You press on—is this going to go on forever?

No answer. Silence. Well that's not good enough. So you climb a tower. You wait. You don't know how long. You refuse to say that what is happening is right. You wait some more.

And finally God answers. But again it is not what you expect. The one who does evil will falter. But the one who does right will live by faithfulness. Faithfulness. Stick-to-it-ness. Perseverance. Heart. You keep plodding along, trusting that in the end God is going to work good for you. But it won't be what you think. Still, just keep on—and live by faith.

You listen some more to God. It is still not what you expect. You wait in the tower in the dark night, in the quiet. You won't give up. Things look terrible now, but you get it. You will turn your own pushiness to effect.

You understand. Even if you see no results, no harvest, no fruit, no food, no animals, only empty barns and empty houses, you will keep on. You will be like David in the cave so long ago. You will continue to praise God no matter what—till the dry dirt fills your mouth. Even when there is no bread, no fruit, and no resources and every option for good is empty.

With determination you will make joy in God the thing you won't give up on. The physical circumstances don't matter. Even how you're feeling doesn't matter.

You will be relentless. You will stubbornly continue to be glad. Somehow that decision changes things. God will make you as determined as a mountain deer, stepping through the rocky places. The places are rocky, but you didn't realize until now that you are on a mountain. In some strange way, the view makes all the difference.

Chapter 12

Constancy

Jeremiah (Jeremiah 15)

Why is my pain unceasing, my wound incurable, refusing to be healed? Will you be to me like a deceitful brook, like waters that fail? Therefore thus says the LORD: "If you return, I will restore you, and you shall stand before me. If you utter what is precious, and not what is worthless, you shall be as my mouth. They shall turn to you, but you shall not turn to them. And I will make you to this people a fortified wall of bronze; they will fight against you, but they shall not prevail over you."

—Jeremiah 15:18–20

No, the view from God's perspective doesn't really make all the difference for you. Not at all. The view actually makes things worse. It looks like everyone hates you, your friends and your enemies. Even your neighbors and relatives in your hometown threaten your life. You've told God more than once you wish you had never been born. You sit alone—no one comforts you. You've had it.

You tell God again. You don't hold back. So you say it. You wish you had *never been born*. All that about calling you before you were formed in your mother's womb. Well, you feel cursed instead of blessed, and you wish you had never been born!

So you ask God more questions. You press Him. Why does the pain just go and on? Yes, you have wounds, but despite the assurances, they never heal. The promises of God? You go ahead and say it in your mind. The *empty* promises of God. Why does the pain continue for so long?

51

But that's not all. You, a prophet of God, a prophet to the nations, no less, press the Almighty with your words. Your experience simply hasn't matched what God promised. You can't lie. If you have learned anything about God, you know you can't lie to Him. He knows your roiling, angry, confused, fearful heart. He knows your love for these people—it is like a parent's love for an ugly child.

You search for the image to express it. Yes, that is it. God has been unreliable. Once you said God was a fountain of living water. But no, the fountain of flowing water has cheated you, deceived you. You, who told others about the fountain, came for water, and there was none there. So you press God, asking, "Is that what You are really like? Yes, that is what You are like. You are like a stream that makes you think there is water in it but is really as dry as dust."

You actually did it. You, the prophet, asked if God was a *liar*, a deceiver. God changed Jacob's name from "Cheater" to "One Who Struggles with God." Has God Himself become the cheater, the deceitful one? You were so sure there would be water in the brook, but there is none.

You wait in silence. Nothing happens for a while. Finally, quietly, firmly, God's word comes to you.

In the past, you have told all the others to repent. But now it is time for *you* to repent. God is not going to destroy you for your unspeakable insolence. God could squash you for your cheekiness in the face of the great vastness of God—with the same harshness He has for the deceitful, prideful people who live in hypocrisy.

Instead he has let you push Him. Now His words are quiet and sure, stabilizing your heart. He says that if you return, He will restore you. Come back, and you can stand before Him once again. You are stunned.

No condemnation, no punishment, no rejection. Calm, firm, steady—God is. Everything you are not. Then His commitment. Your emotions go up and down like the waves. But God says He will make you into a wall, fortified, not of wood or brick but of bronze. A thick metal wall—they can't even put a dent in you. Sturdy, firm, constant, unfailing—tough. And in the end, all those who hate you, all those who are trying to kill you—they will not prevail. You will learn not to be afraid when the heat comes.

That's God's promise after all your questions and pushing and accusations. Will you believe him even when the others hate you?

Chapter 13

Pluck

The Roof-Splitter (Mark 2:1–12)

And many were gathered together, so that there was no more room, not even at the door. And he was preaching the word to them. And they came, bringing to him a paralytic carried by four men. *And when they could not get near him because of the crowd, they removed the roof above him, and when they had made an opening, they let down the bed on which the paralytic lay.* And when Jesus saw their faith, he said to the paralytic, "Son, your sins are forgiven." Now some of the scribes were sitting there, questioning in their hearts, "Why does this man speak like that? He is blaspheming! Who can forgive sins but God alone?" And immediately Jesus, perceiving in his spirit that they thus questioned within themselves, said to them, "Why do you question these things in your hearts? Which is easier, to say to the paralytic, 'Your sins are forgiven,' or to say, 'Rise, take up your bed and walk'? But that you may know that the Son of Man has authority on earth to forgive sins"—he said to the paralytic—"I say to you, rise, pick up your bed, and go home." And he rose and immediately picked up his bed and went out before them all, so that they were all amazed and glorified God, saying, "We never saw anything like this!"

—Mark 2:2–12

You don't care if the crowd gets mad; you don't care even if they hate you. No way you are giving up now. You and your buddies have carried your sick friend on a mat all this way. You've heard all about Jesus. He can fix your friend. Yes, you had to stop on the way to rest, especially when you tripped and almost dropped him. Your friend didn't say much. He wasn't one of those guys who shouted to be careful after the fact—after a fellow had messed up.

Yes, it was hot, and, yes, you started sweating. But if your friend on the mat could be fixed, well, that would change everything—just to see him once more the way he used to be, not all whipped and skinny and quiet the way he is in these hot days.

But now that you've gotten to the house where Jesus is your heart sinks. People are crowded everywhere. It's like a mob. You were not the only ones with this idea. Some are using crutches, some are blind, some are pressing against the doors just to catch a glimpse of Jesus or hear His voice. There's no line, there's no movement, no process, no way to get in. Just a lot of noise and people jostling each other to get a better position to hear.

Don't give up. Don't give up. You and your buddies put your friend down on the road gently. There's always a plan B. And a plan C and a plan D—however many plans it takes. Your friend on the mat looks at you with a hopeless look. There is no way . . . he seems to be thinking. You look back at him with a frown. No, there's no way we are going to give up. It's not time to go home yet, not until your friend is fixed.

You're a practical man. Let other people shout challenges to God. You just need to get your friend to Jesus—you've heard what He can do. You can't get through the door or through any other possible opening in the house. People are crowded everywhere, thick as frantic flies. You look up. At the matting on the roof. It could be removed, with a little work and a little know-how, at least enough to get your friend through. Sure, it's a risk. But you've got to take a risk sometimes.

You gather your buddies around and pool your resources—clothing and straps. You find some rope behind the house. This contraption with the mat isn't going to be pretty. The crowd doesn't pay any attention to you. They have other things on their minds. No, it isn't elegant, but you can find a way because you're doing it for your pal.

Jesus is still speaking, and the crowd is still pressing in everywhere. With a little effort and grunting you make it to the roof. Easy does it, guys. Don't slip. This can be done. You have put on roofs before. You dig out the material on the flat roof carefully and lay it aside. Now you can see into the house. A little bit of the roofing has dropped through, and every face is looking up as you make the hole bigger and bigger. You are right above the one who is talking. That must be Jesus.

You can't stop now. One man in the room below looks particularly upset. Maybe it is his house. Those other hot shots, the lawyers and teachers, don't look too happy either. No matter. The hole gets bigger and bigger. You work as quickly as you can, and your buddies all help. There. Big enough to get your pal through. Easy does it, guys. Here we go. Keep everything level. You don't want him to drop now.

Total silence on the inside. Talk about dramatic entrances. Everyone makes room as your friend is lowered. It's working like a charm. Now Jesus is standing right beside him. You and your buddies are all on your hands and knees on the roof, sticking your heads through the hole like a bunch of hand puppets.

Now what will Jesus say? Will He be mad that His perfect teaching has been interrupted, perhaps at the most important point? Maybe you did the wrong thing. Maybe He thinks you cheated and have been way too pushy. Maybe He thinks you cut in line. Well, you did. What if He is angry and curses your friend instead of fixing him? His words seem to be very powerful. Too late to wonder about that now.

Jesus looks up at you four, looking silly with your heads sticking through the hole in the roof. The cramped moment seems to go on and on. Then Jesus gives a sort-of smile. You let out a long breath.

Jesus turns to your friend, lying at His feet. What is He saying? "Son"? Your friend is not His son. Did Jesus just say his sins were forgiven? How did He know all that about your friend? You hadn't told Him. Can He really do that? Forgive sins like He is God? You look at your friend's face down there on the mat. His face has changed. He doesn't look hopeless any more.

You can't hear the next part of the discussion. It gets pretty lively, and Jesus faces the hotshots in the crowd now. He turns to your friend again and says something pretty loud and strong. You can hear it from the roof. Jesus told him to take up his mat and walk. The crowd is totally silent. Nothing happens. No, something is happening. Your pal, your buddy who hasn't moved for months, stirs a little bit. You can't speak. There's this big lump in your throat.

Yes, you can see it. Your best friend moves one of his feet.

Chapter 14

Gumption

The Outsider (Matthew 15:21–28)

And Jesus went away from there and withdrew to the district of Tyre and Sidon. And behold, a Canaanite woman from that region came out and was crying, "Have mercy on me, O Lord, Son of David; my daughter is severely oppressed by a demon." But he did not answer her a word. And his disciples came and begged him, saying, "Send her away, for she is crying out after us." He answered, "I was sent only to the lost sheep of the house of Israel." But she came and knelt before him, saying, "Lord, help me." And he answered, "It is not right to take the children's bread and throw it to the dogs." *She said, "Yes, Lord, yet even the dogs eat the crumbs that fall from their masters' table." Then Jesus answered her, "O woman, great is your faith! Be it done for you as you desire."* And her daughter was healed instantly.

—Matthew 15:21–28

You've heard the extravagant stories about Him. You've heard about those guys on the roof. That took guts. You've heard about how He helped even the Romans—He even healed a Roman soldier's servant. But what has happened to you now doesn't really surprise you.

They ignore you. You don't even exist. You know they don't really hate you. It is just that you are invisible. And they don't even know your name. You're a nothing. A Canaanite. A woman. You don't know about those people they talk about—Job or Jacob or Moses or Abraham or any of that stuff. If you try to make yourself visible, they will just find you irritating.

But you can only think about your daughter, your little one. She's not the baby you raised and sang to and coddled. She's breaking your heart. She's possessed by something that isn't her. She strikes out at you, at everyone. As you walk, all you can see is her writhing on the floor at home, groaning in pain. It's as though someone has torn your insides out and thrown them on the street.

But you've got gumption. You've heard of him. You have tried everything else. You can't take her with you. She can't even function in public anymore.

So you walk. Miles and miles and miles. Men on the road try to make eye contact with you. You sleep one night next to a wall to keep out of the wind and, more importantly, out of sight. At midnight it rains.

But as you walk, you hear more people talk. People are being forgiven. People are starting over again. Most of all, people are being healed.

You ask for directions fearlessly. Finally you see Him. You know because there is a crowd around Him, and His special followers stay close by. You try to come up to Him, but the crowd is too much. You can't get close enough to Him for Him to even hear you. Besides, you are a Canaanite, a foreigner, and a woman.

The people disregard you, give you that vague look like you are unclean. And they all have their own needs. They are not thinking about you. A wave of disappointment and exhaustion passes over you. It's hopeless. You can't even get near Him. You think about turning around and going home.

But you don't care. You see your daughter in your mind, a harsh image, there on the floor at home, groaning. He is passing you by, and then you will have nothing. So you shout. "Have mercy on me, O Lord!" You shout some more, spit flying from your mouth, saying whatever you think can get through. You call him the Son of David. You know that much, but not much more. You won't quit.

Jesus doesn't turn around. He doesn't say a word to you. You are aware of how much you are annoying His followers. They want His attention too. Jesus keeps walking.

Tough. You can keep shouting. Louder and louder. You make a scene. It is the only thing you know to do.

The followers go to Jesus and speak intently. You know they are talking about you, that you've become a kind of problem. You hate that feeling. But so what? Jesus says something back to the followers and keeps walking. This is a little unexpected. He's not going to come to you after all, even after the commotion you have made. Whatever He said, the followers closest to Him seem to agree. Things don't look good for you.

So you ratchet things up a notch. You run ahead of Him now, pushing people aside as you go. You get in front of Him and fall to your knees— you make it dramatic, so He has to stop. You look up at His face. It wasn't the face you expected—relentless but kind, and with questioning eyes, curious yet very determined.

You are so exhausted, so disappointed, you can't speak. For a moment, you croak like a frog. All you can think of is your precious daughter. What she was like as a baby. Holding her in your arms and singing to her. Bathing her, nursing her, laughing when she learned to walk. All you can bleat out is, "Lord help me."

The bustle stops. What Jesus says is a like a slap in your face. All is lost.

He speaks to you and uses a comparison. "It is not fair to take the children's bread and throw it to the dogs." You understand. He called you a dog. A familiar term for those not of His kind. You have been insulted, and this is your cue to leave. You won't get anything. You can tell the crowd completely agrees. Some of them actually nod their heads.

You look at His serious face and see the slightest turn of his eyes, as though He is playing, testing you. Well, two can play this game. You don't have much, but you've got gumption. So you fight back. "Yes, but even the dogs eat the crumbs that fall from the master's table." You say it with all the confidence you can muster.

Everyone is quiet now, annoyed by the impudence from this foreigner. He looks at you for a long time, studying your face. You notice the slightest of smiles. "You've won," he says, but not in words. Finally he says, "O woman, great is your faith! Be it done for you as you desire."

You didn't feel anything. You walked the long way home, numb. Why did He say what he said? Why did He make it so hard at the first? Why did He make you feel as though it were some kind of contest? You don't quite understand. You only know your daughter is quietly sitting in a chair when you got home.

Chapter 15

Persistence

Jesus (Luke 11 and 18; Mark 8)

And he said to them, "Which of you who has a friend will go to him at midnight and say to him, 'Friend, lend me three loaves, for a friend of mine has arrived on a journey, and I have nothing to set before him'; and he will answer from within, 'Do not bother me; the door is now shut, and my children are with me in bed. I cannot get up and give you anything'? I tell you, though he will not get up and give him anything because he is his friend, *yet because of his impudence he will rise and give him whatever he needs.*"

Luke 11:5–8

And he told them a parable to the effect that they ought always to pray and not lose heart. He said, "In a certain city there was a judge who neither feared God nor respected man. And there was a widow in that city who kept coming to him and saying, 'Give me justice against my adversary.' For a while he refused, but afterward he said to himself, 'Though I neither fear God nor respect man, *yet because this widow keeps bothering me, I will give her justice, so that she will not beat me down by her continual coming.*'"

Luke 18:1–5

And he began to teach them that the Son of Man must suffer many things and be rejected by the elders and the chief priests and the scribes and be killed, and after three days rise again.

And he said this plainly. And *Peter took him aside and began to rebuke him.*

Mark 8:31–32

That precious mother from Canaan understood more than she knew. You wonder if Your own mother will understand. These ones certainly don't.

They still don't understand. Your followers look at You with those eager and blank faces. They think prayer is like a magic show. That is all they see. They don't understand that the whole thing is something more than faith. How do you get through to them that now you are talking more about faithfulness than some quick-fix idea? Words fail.

So you try stories. No matter what, their faces take on more focus if you tell a story. So when they ask you about prayer, you tell a story about a man who is fast asleep in the middle of the night. You act it out. You use different voices. You snore deeply. They think this is funny, and they all point to Peter. You tell them about a neighbor who needs three loaves of bread at midnight.

More acting out. You knock on an old piece of wood as loud as you can. You pretend to be the sleeping man, almost opening his eyes, but then thinks better of it and goes back to sleep. They laugh. More knocking, louder, shouting outside from the neighbor. The sleeping man won't get up. So more knocking on the door, louder, shouting from outside. The sleeping man rubs his eyes and finally shouts, "What? What is it?" More knocking on the old door.

You wait to see if they understand. They don't. You spell it out a little. The sleeping man won't give the neighbor bread because of friendship. Now you wait, you don't go too fast. It's better if they get it on their own. Let them struggle with it a bit. You get quiet now, after all the acting out—shouting and knocking and irritated grumbling. You finally say, "Impudence. It is his persistent impudence that does it."

They get it, but they don't. You watch a few squint their eyes and look out at the scrubby trees. "Are you comparing God to a sleepy, grouchy man at midnight who doesn't honor friendship?" You see it in their eyes.

Good. They are thinking. They are fighting to make sense of it. You don't say anything else. You want them to work on this—"How much more would God . . . ?" You let it go for now.

But You aren't finished about prayer. "Ask and keep on asking," You say. "Seek and keep on seeking." You knock on the piece of wood again over and over. Maybe they will remember that. "Knock and keep on knock-ing and keep on knocking." Enough. Let them think about it some more. They won't remember it unless you let them mull it over on their own and come to a conclusion. You move on to other subjects.

But they still don't understand. On another day You circle around to this again, when you talk about prayer again. They don't comprehend how important this is. Another story—make it disturbing, or they won't remember it. They still don't perceive that losing heart, quitting when it gets tough, is the worst thing that can happen when you pray. Quitting blocks what God can do.

Once upon a time, You say, there was an evil judge, unscrupulous, doing everything for the bribe. He didn't believe in God, and he didn't care what people thought either. Their eyes brighten up already.

You act it out again. The judge, bored, pompous, self-centered. Then You act out the part of the widow. They love this. You creep along like an old woman, but a persistent, tough old irritating woman. They under-stand. Many have tried to get something fairly and seen that it doesn't work. You push your way to the imaginary judge acting out the part of this woman. You use an old woman's voice.

You tell them she keeps coming over and over and over and over again. She is tiresome, obnoxious. The judge can't stand her. You get them laughing.

Finally the judge rolls his eyes and says, "I don't care about God or people. I certainly don't care about this annoying old woman's case. But because she is continually bothering me, I will resolve her case so that she will *leave me alone!*"

You wait a bit. You look at your followers' blank faces. They are trying to get it, but they don't. Peter is about to speak and challenge You.

You say, "Won't God make things right for His chosen ones, who cry out day and night?"

You wait again. It is dawning on them. Is Jesus comparing God to this evil, wicked judge? That doesn't seem right.

Good. It is upsetting them. Maybe it will rock the boat of their thoughts. They've got to learn about spunk, about grit—what that annoying old lady had, what Jacob in the Torah had. You finish with a question and leave it at that for now. "When the Son of Man comes, will He find faith on earth?" You are hoping they are beginning to think "faithfulness" when you talk about faith, but you can't be sure by the way they look at you. They still don't understand.

Peter struggles most of all with it. You tell the disciples in every way possible that winning will sometimes look like losing. Anyone could see that going to Jerusalem this last time will be a confrontation with worldly forces that have the power to destroy. It's inevitable if You go there this time. Good old Peter. He takes You aside to instruct You on what is right. He puts his arm around You like an older brother. He rebukes You for saying You will be beaten, mocked, and killed. You are a lot of things, he says in his own way, but not a loser.

You respond strongly. But in the end, it won't be Your words that will convince them. It would be easy, and tempting, not to go. Couldn't You just stay here and keep teaching them—just keep telling stories?

But You set your face toward Jerusalem, the place of religious and political power. You won't be turned aside. They follow, with no

comprehension and sometimes looking stunned. They can't understand why You, the Messiah, would give in to these worldly forces when
You don't have to. They can't understand why You would let the enemies of God's people, the Romans, kill You, triumph over You. For them,
it is unthinkable.

So You keep on, Your face as hard as stone. Eventually they will learn
about how to hold on and when to give in, You hope. That's the whole
point of life, knowing how to hold on and when to give in. Will Peter get
it? What about Your own mom? Will she understand when things get
hard?

Chapter 16

Heart

Mary (John 19)

So the soldiers did these things, but *standing by the cross of Jesus were his mother and his mother's sister*, Mary the wife of Clopas, and Mary Magdalene. When Jesus saw his mother and the disciple whom he loved standing nearby, he said to his mother, "Woman, behold, your son!" Then he said to the disciple, "Behold, your mother!"

—John 19:24–27

What could be worse than a parent surviving her own child? Watching your child die.

What is worse than watching your child die? Watching your child be killed before your eyes.

What is worse than watching your own child be killed before your eyes? Watching Him be tortured and mocked before being killed.

What is worse than watching your child be tortured? Watching Him be tortured when there is nothing you can do to help Him. Hour after hour.

They wake you in the middle of the night and tell you your son has been arrested. This is not a complete surprise. You get up and put your clothes on, though you can't speak, and you can hardly breathe.

You know Him. You know what He is planning to do. He will not run, resist, or give in. He is so determined. And you know what they will do also. It is unspeakable.

You know what an execution is like. You have seen it so many times along the road between Nazareth and Jerusalem. You have never been able to look into the faces of the ones hanging by the road in agony. You have always thought that each one of these poor men was at one time someone's little baby, regardless of how wretched they look now.

For some reason you think of your own son's little hands as an infant, grasping your finger as He nursed. Your first child. You think of Him as a baby, looking so quizzically at His tiny hands, discovering each finger. Then you think of a huge nail piercing that hand. It can't be.

John's face has a look of terror on it. He will walk with you and your sister to try to find out what is happening. You gather that all of the disciples ran away, all of them, even John. Why didn't John stay and help Him? You stay quiet. Maybe it is all a mistake. Maybe they have already released Him. Maybe He will walk in the door any minute, well and smiling at this close brush with death, just as He has done before.

But you know it won't be like that this time. You're His mother, and you know Him. You refuse to let your mind imagine the beating, the blood, the bruises, the excrement, the nakedness—His precious body suspended on a pole designed for torture. You refuse. You turn your eyes upward. How can anyone, anyone, be asked to do what you are being pressed to do? It's inconceivable. But you are dead set on being there.

So you take a deep breath, and you take John's arm, and you go. You will not leave your son. You will stay there to the end, whatever comes.

Chapter 17

Staying Power

Peter (John 21)

When they had finished breakfast, Jesus said to Simon Peter, "Simon, son of John, do you love me more than these?" He said to him, "Yes, Lord; you know that I love you." He said to him, "Feed my lambs." He said to him a second time, "Simon, son of John, do you love me?" He said to him, "Yes, Lord; you know that I love you." He said to him, "Tend my sheep." He said to him the third time, "Simon, son of John, do you love me?" *Peter was grieved because he said to him the third time, "Do you love me?" and he said to him, "Lord, you know everything; you know that I love you."* Jesus said to him, "Feed my sheep. Truly, truly, I say to you, when you were young, you used to dress yourself and walk wherever you wanted, but when you are old, you will stretch out your hands, and another will dress you and carry you where you do not want to go."

—John 21:15–18

Yes, you ran away when the worst happened. You didn't even think about His own mother until much later.

Will you ever learn? About not giving up and about when to give in? He changed your name, just the way God changed Jacob's name—Jacob, who had to struggle so much. Your new name? Rock. Strong and stable as a rock. What a joke. It doesn't feel that way today. You were just like all the other disciples when everything fell apart—you ran like a rabbit. You, the one who was as sturdy as a stone, who warmed your hands at the enemy's fire, wouldn't even admit you knew Him, and you did it three times.

Three times. You claimed you would take a stand for the Messiah, but you didn't. When the crowd didn't agree with you around the embers, when their eyes turned to exclude, when you were alone without any other support, you caved in. You didn't want to get crucified. None of the disciples did.

And here He is again, on your turf, smiling, making breakfast. The whole world has changed. You are so very happy, and still, you cannot look Him in the eye. You focus on eating another piece of fish.

"Do you love Me?" He asks. Now He has put his finger on the problem, right in front of the other disciples. You fumble with a fishbone.

"Yes, Lord, you know I love you." It felt as though His words were cutting into your heart. You were so ashamed of your failure.

"Then feed My lambs"

Yes, an assignment. Something to do. You would do anything, anywhere, anytime. Whew. It is over. Now Jesus can talk to some of the other disciples and challenge them. You can move on. You are so desperate to forget all that happened in the previous weeks.

But Jesus is not through. He presses harder. He asks the same question again. Everyone knows what He is talking about. Peter, Rock—you were the leader. Why is Jesus asking you a second time? Why is He pushing you in this way? Doesn't He know how awkward this is for you?

You respond again. You say the same thing. You sense He is probing, and it hurts. It's like a physician cutting something out that could infect the whole body.

Jesus gives you the same assignment. Got it. Enough said. No need to continue. Let's change the subject and talk about some of the other disciples. What about John, for instance?

But Jesus asks again, probing, pushing—the same question. It's as though He is applying more pressure just to see what you are made of. What can you say? Each time the words hurt even more. All you can do is be honest. He knows it all anyway. You love Him, you love Him, you love Him—even though you failed so miserably in the time He needed you most. It's all out in the open. Your sorrow and shame is horrid. Yes, you denied you knew Him three times.

And now, for the third time, He gives you the same assignment. But this time He says more. You, who are self-willed and as stubborn as a mule, will be led to places you don't want to go. And that, in the end, is how you are going to die.

You are going to have to be tough. Like a rock. And you are going to have to be honest. Every time you share with others, let them know how you failed in the time when Jesus needed you most. And tell them how He pressed you, asking again and again the same question and how He gave you the assignment not because of your achievements, but in spite of them.

You think about Judas—he fell through too, and then he killed himself. And what about yourself? Is it possible the one who fails and gets up is stronger than the one who never fails? Maybe that is what Jesus was probing for, over and over—for what you are made of after one, after two, after three or more failures. Maybe He was doing something more for you than just making an awkward moment in front of the others.

Well, no matter what, you are sticking with Him. Even if you fail in the future. Where else can you go? Once again He has the words of life. As you toyed with your fish, He was really building you up. Sounds like you are going to need that.

Chapter 18

Determination

Paul (1 Timothy 6; 2 Timothy 4)

But as for you, O man of God, flee these things. Pursue righteousness, godliness, faith, love, steadfastness, gentleness. *Fight the good fight of the faith.* Take hold of the eternal life to which you were called and about which you made the good confession in the presence of many witnesses.

—1 Timothy 6:11–12

For I am already being poured out as a drink offering, and the time of my departure has come. *I have fought the good fight, I have finished the race, I have kept the faith.*

—2 Timothy 4:6–7

You know the stories about Peter and the other disciples of Jesus—how they didn't understand and how they failed. Of course they didn't understand, and of course they failed. So did you.

Now you think you apprehend a bit more, even though in this life it will always be a little murky. You talk about the peace of God when you write your letters, but you also write that it's a fight. It's just not what you thought at the beginning. Earlier in your life you felt that it was a fight against people—arresting them, killing them, defeating them. That must mean you win.

Once you thought it was that kind of fight. Now you see it's not a fight against flesh and blood, but it's not really a fight against circumstances or habits either. It's another kind of fight—it's the fight to believe.

What is faith? You know in your heart it's the determination to see God's invisible love through these puzzling visible circumstances—this imprisonment, this rejection. It's a kind of fight of faith. It's the fight to rest in God's good promises through Christ and to not give up. Jacob understood. "I won't let You go until You bless me," he had said.

You're still learning step-by-step about this kind of faith. It is a type of single-minded faith to trust what is coming. It's a faith that can be content when things go up or when things go down, even when there is a struggle. It's faithfulness. In all these changes you trust in the deepest sense that God will work all things for good through Christ, who loves you and gave Himself for you.

You push Timothy. He's like a son to you. He's got to have that grit too. "Fight the good fight of faith," you say. You keep talking to him. "Don't let anyone write you off because you are young, or because you are sick, or because you are unable. Don't do it! Show some pluck—like Abraham, like Jacob, like Jesus. Sure there are some tough things. A baby may be protected, but a fighter must take some hits. And you are a fighter."

As for yourself, things aren't so great for you now. So what? You've been in jail before. When you came before the court all the people you thought would stand by you deserted you. The dashed hopes and exhaustion hit you like a wave. And then Alexander, your own fellow Christian, betrayed you and hurt you terribly.

After all these years. After all your work, the sweat, and the travel. It still shocks you to see your own hands, the deep veins, the knobby knuckles, the hands of an old man. Oh well. Do these others who deserted you know what it is like? You had a mob corner you and throw large stones at you. Do they know what it is like to be knocked unconscious, to wake up hearing the mumbling of a guilty crowd as it recedes? Don't just lie there, you said to yourself. Get up. Jesus was always telling people to get up, lame people, paralyzed people, and they did. So you've been stoned. You're not dead. Get up. So you did.

Do these others know what it is like to hold on to a piece of wood for a day and a night in the water, soaked and half dead, muscles aching, with nothing but just a little more determination to hang on for one more hour, one more moment?

Do they know what it is like to have your own people whip you, your own people—the sour humiliation of it all. These are the people you trained with—the people of the Word, the people who claim to treasure God's teaching.

You didn't have to be here. You could have been in Jerusalem, respected, bending to their ways, honored, comfortable. Not here in this dungeon, treated like a common criminal.

You try to tell Timothy—so young. Does he have the backbone to do this, the patience? You've tried so many times to put this into words for him, and you have still failed. Bottom line—you fight. You can't be a jellyfish. You learn to fight by facing hard things, over and over and over again. If a snake bites you, you don't curl up and die. Sometimes you've just got to shake it off and keep going.

Then you don't only fight, you can fight like crazy. Resistance has a way of making your faith stronger. Like a boxer who strikes his own body to prepare himself, his muscles and bones get tougher.

But then, you are not fighting to win—it's not yet the way that Timothy still sees the world so often. Christ showed this other astonishing way. The Way. Through your whole life, you can't get over the wonder of it.

All those opponents—you are not fighting to win *over* them. You are fighting to win them over. It's the same way He won you over. He appeared to you on the road when you were His enemy. And instead of destroying you, He didn't hesitate to ask you to join Him. And you did.

So, in a sense, you are really fighting to lose. You could probably find some way to beat your own people, using power, influence, resources, and intellect. Instead you fight in ways that make you look defeated. You are whipped, beaten, stoned, or imprisoned—like you are again now. You certainly don't look like a winner. Will Timothy understand?

You didn't really understand until you understood Jesus' loss. He lost so terribly, so horribly, so appallingly. The powers of the world thought His undoing meant the death of His way and the victory of theirs, but the world was wrong. They didn't understand God's terrible tenderness, His relentless, terrible tenderness, going to any lengths for us.

So you continue on, following this other way. You win over the Gentiles, the Hebrews, even your fellow competing Christians, by fighting to lose. Does Timothy really comprehend that when he is weak, then he is strong? This isn't a giving-up weakness, a quitting weakness, a can't-take-it weakness. No. It is about determination, tenacity, grit *in order to* be weak. Like Christ—*determined* to be crucified in weakness. He would not allow the angels to save Him. You want Timothy to understand this different kind of power, this inverted, reversed, upside-down, inside-out, backward strength—strength to lose so that others can really win.

But you can't be with Timothy now. In the end, you find yourself in jail—again. Deserted by your friends, old, poor, cold. You have to ask for your coat. You've got to smile. You're not exactly who you thought you'd become when you thought about it as a young man. You just want Timothy to get the picture and to see how right and how wonderful it is. Many people start strong—lots of them. You want Timothy to stay the course, to refuse to quit.

You think about the first disciples and what they understood. You wonder if Peter is still alive. James—you know he is dead. You haven't heard about John for a while. He was always so much gentler than you are. You wonder how he is doing.

Chapter 19

Resolve

John (Revelation 1)

> I, John, your brother and partner in the tribulation and the kingdom and the patient endurance that are in Jesus, was on the island called Patmos on account of the word of God and the testimony of Jesus. *I was in the Spirit on the Lord's day, and I heard behind me a loud voice like a trumpet saying,* "Write what you see in a book and send it to the seven churches, to Ephesus and to Smyrna and to Pergamum and to Thyatira and to Sardis and to Philadelphia and to Laodicea."
>
> —Revelation 1:9–11

Now you're old. Really old. Most of the other disciples, the ones who walked with you with Jesus, well—they have all died or been killed. But they haven't been able to kill you yet. Each morning you wake up on this island in exile and look out across the water to the sunrise. So much water, so much separation from your friends, the church, your community, your former life. So much you would like to say to them, but you can't.

It feels as though all you have now are your memories, those memories that will leave this earth when you leave this earth. The disciples, the crowds, the groups huddled in houses, the miracles, His face, and most of all His words—His deep, deep words, so simple and sometimes so puzzling, but with so much meaning. The older you get, the more they mean. You can go back over them again and again and again, and each time you get something more from them. His words, His words are like a well you can draw water from. You remember those words, and they are still fresh. And now, everything around you—the sky, the birds, the sea, this sunrise—are all seen through His words.

You've learned a few things along the way. You wish you had a way to say it. Here you are, elderly and in exile, but you remember what it was like to be young. You didn't understand then. Some of the things you thought were mansions turned out to be caves, and some of the things you thought were caves turned out to be mansions.

What does it mean to grow old? It means to refuse to give up, to be relentless in refusing to give up, to continue regardless of the challenges, until a certain kind of resolve rises in you. It's a resolve that knows in the midst of the storm the firmness inside of you is still there. And even when the firmness is not there, you still say, "I won't let You go unless You bless me."

You have seen old people, angry at the disappointments, the failure of their bodies, cynical, resentful, unhappy, despairing. You could be that way too, with all the deaths you have seen. He was crucified when He was still fairly young, but He prepared you. No one takes your life from you. You lay it down—so He said, willingly, at the right time. No sense in being angry at life, the system, the people who brought you here to this island and this exile. That way, the way of anger, will only make you something you were never meant to be, even if all the injustices are true. There is another way—He showed you—they weren't just rules. He Himself was that way.

The pettiness of things here—getting water for the day, managing scraps of food, just keeping the body together. But you are going to finish strong. You aren't going to give up now, just because you are imprisoned on this island. Something inside of you rises up and makes you stronger. Your friends, Peter, James, Jesus, Paul—you won't give up on them either. It takes a certain kind of persistence to get this old, a persistent refusal to get surly, petty, or self-centered.

It takes a certain kind of persistence to keep praying as you grow old too. When you close your eyes, so many victories and setbacks flood your heart. Things that never happened that should have happened. Hopes that turned into something else. The people who have died—some so unfairly. But every morning you look out at the water and you pray. When you are quiet, you can even see the thread of love that moves through the memories, both the victories and the supposed failures.

The supposed failures. You remember—He is the light, and in Him there is no darkness at all. Day after day in exile on this island. You will need to be tough to be prayerful now, even to see just a little bit.

Then one Sunday—the Lord's Day—just after sunrise, you were worship-ping alone, and you heard a voice. It sounded like a trumpet. It was so clear and loud. And when you turned, even though your hearing is dull and your eyes are dim, you *really* started to see.

Part 2

Relenting

You are familiar with the generosity of our Master, Jesus Christ. Rich as he was, he gave it all away for us—in one stroke he became poor and we became rich.

—2 Corinthians 8:9 *The Message*

For you know the grace of our Lord Jesus Christ, that though he was rich, yet for your sake he became poor, so that you by his poverty might become rich.

—2 Corinthians 8:9

Chapter 20

Surrendering

John (Revelation 5:1–8)

> Then I saw in the right hand of him who was seated on the throne a scroll written within and on the back, sealed with seven seals. And I saw a mighty angel proclaiming with a loud voice, "Who is worthy to open the scroll and break its seals?" And no one in heaven or on earth or under the earth was able to open the scroll or to look into it, and I began to weep loudly because no one was found worthy to open the scroll or to look into it. And one of the elders said to me, "Weep no more; behold, the Lion of the tribe of Judah, the Root of David, has conquered, so that he can open the scroll and its seven seals." And *between the throne and the four living creatures and among the elders I saw a Lamb standing, as though it had been slain.*
>
> —Revelation 5:1–6

Some mornings, when John looks out at the sunrise over the water, he feels as though they have lost. He's seen the death of so many friends. The ranks of his companions are so much thinner. Sometimes he thinks, as he grows older, that he lives more and more with ghosts. All the memories of people no longer here, after such a long life. The younger ones don't remember. He's learned enough to keep his mouth shut much of the time when he is with the young ones. He is careful when he talks with them about how he walked with Me in the past. His words are on the present—what I am doing now. Good for him.

So I came to him in his prayer on a Sunday. I wanted him to understand. These agonizing contradictions in life. Sometimes it is better to put the contradictions into pictures, visions so to speak—better that way than to put them into words.

I gave him pictures and sound and a drama that seemed so wide to him—a vision. In the vision, the loud voice asks across heaven and earth—who is able to unlock and interpret the meaning of the dance of humanity, its heartache and its joy? Who is able to open that scroll?

Nothing but silence. Nothing but silence across the whole universe of humankind and creatures and angels. Nothing but that familiar silence for a long, long time. It is a like a dream, this vision, and like a dream the emotions can be achingly intense. Then there is a sound, the sound of a man weeping. John himself cries, and well he should. His heart touches, for just a moment, the tragic music of the human story—it makes Me weep too. No one on earth is able, no one is worthy, no one can interpret. No philosopher or scientist or poet or angel has ever *really* made plain the heartbreaking riddle of human existence, though many have tried. Life remains locked, unopened, a sealed book.

John understands this. For all their songs, for all their joy, his brothers and sisters continue to die, continue to be locked up, continue to have their property and family taken away. Some prayers are wonderfully answered, and then, for him, some are not. But it is more than that. The shell of life itself isn't yet cracked open. No one can quite see the kernel.

John wants to see. In the vision, I send a wise one, an elder to speak to him, to comfort him, to nudge him a little further down the road. In the silence, he puts his hand on John's shoulder, and tells him not to cry anymore. The elder describes Me as one with power and uses the language John has heard all his life and can understand. The Lion of Judah, the predicted Messiah, the special one, kingly, powerful, able to conquer, able to destroy enemies, able to triumph. This is the one who will triumph over the authorities and all the powers that be, all the ones that seem to be winning despite so many faithful petitions. This is the one who can open the scroll.

But here is where I turn things inside out once again for John. There in the middle of the throne and the elders, I give him an image, a vision, but not what the world expected, not a lion after all. I give him an image of a little animal. A small, wounded lamb.

Will he understand? Will he ever really understand the difference between winning and losing? Does he see what it costs? He heard Me called a lamb at the beginning when he was young. Did he know how resolute one must be in order to be a lamb?

People must be relentless in their love in order to be relenting. It will take extreme perseverance to learn when to give in for someone else out of love.

Even here John will still have to choose—apparent superiority, like a lion, or sacrifice, like a lamb. Should he have a wider compass and physical freedom, like a lion, or stricter confinement and fewer options, like a lamb? He has to choose every day. Here on this island his jailers might quickly give him freedom, if he would only relent on certain things.

Poor John. He has been pushed through so much. He has outlived the others. I've told him the same things before, in different ways. I told him about laying down My life; no one could take it from Me. He looks ahead—will he be able to share My heart to others in words once more? Will he be able to say, while he is still trapped on an island in the middle of this blue sea, that the deepest part of God is not a lion after all but one who is willing to be small and to be wounded?

Will he be able to see, even now in his loneliness, that love without sacrifice becomes something else? Without sacrifice, even love only becomes another acquisition at someone else's expense. So many of My children have it wrong—working to acquire things, including love. But in the end, this work never fulfills. One grows old, and dies, and celebrates mere conquest—a hollow victory at the end of life, the victory of a mere lion.

As for me, I am often losing in order to win. I lost the battle in the garden for the heart of Adam and Eve, but it was just the beginning. I lost my precious ones in the wilderness, but I didn't give up. I lost my people many times, but I kept coming back. I looked like a loser when I was crucified. It looked like the oppressors had won again. My followers often look like losers. Will John understand now? He's seen so much. Will he turn now for help from the lion, or will he still cling to the lamb?

Yes, yes. He stops weeping. He looks out at the bright water around him that stretches to the horizon, and then he closes his eyes. He has no more tears.

Chapter 21

Offering

Paul (1 Timothy 6; 2 Corinthians 13)

But as for you, O man of God, flee these things. Pursue righteousness, godliness, faith, love, steadfastness, gentleness. *Fight the good fight of the faith.* Take hold of the eternal life to which you were called and about which you made the good confession in the presence of many witnesses.

—1 Timothy 6:11–12

Since you seek proof that Christ is speaking in me. He is not weak in dealing with you, but is powerful among you. *For he was crucified in weakness, but lives by the power of God. For we also are weak in him, but in dealing with you we will live with him by the power of God.* Examine yourselves, to see whether you are in the faith. Test yourselves. Or do you not realize this about yourselves, that Jesus Christ is in you?—unless indeed you fail to meet the test!

—2 Corinthians 13:3–5

I spoke to John in a way that was different from the way I spoke to Paul. I just love Paul for what he is. Sure, he can be a little pushy sometimes, a little sarcastic even. But he's scrappy. He's not a quitter; he's a fighter. Someone like Paul or Jacob holds a special place in my heart—someone who simply doesn't give up. And difficulties aren't necessarily bad. They can strengthen a person's faith like labor strengthens the body. People often really change through the challenge, not through the deliverance.

Strong people stand up for themselves, but stronger people stand up for others. Paul said just the right thing to Timothy, just when Timothy was feeling the weakest. Of course Paul had no idea people would be reading his letter thousands of years later. That's merely the way life is—so many unintended consequences people never realize, and they won't know in their time on earth. The steps to help just one other person walk with Me has so many ripples people will never see.

Sometimes I see Paul really started to understand. Like the letters he wrote to the church at Corinth. Things were so turbulent, and My children said so many things about Paul. Poor fellow. He felt defeated, crushed, overwhelmed, ready to quit. He didn't realize how well he was doing, at the very time he was feeling the worst. As it often happens, when the pressure was on, he got a deeper insight—one tiny baby step further to comprehending.

When his opponents started bragging about their spiritual strengths, My Paul began bragging about his spiritual *weakness*—getting let down in a basket to escape, praying three times and *not* getting what he asked for. He saw that a certain kind of competitiveness in the kingdom of God just becomes another kind of game. It has the same rules as the rest of the world, comparing talents, tallying the score, getting anxious to see who is most popular.

He came back again to My way. Crucified not in strength, not like a winner in the world's eyes, but in weakness. It doesn't take someone who is brilliant to see that from the world's view, being crucified by the oppressors of God's people is considered losing. Total naked failure.

For each person, following Me always means loss. Sacrifice, by its very nature, means loss. No real long-term love can thrive without some relinquishment, something that is given up.

The church there in Corinth was filled with the spirit of victory, but things had gotten a little twisted. It took a while for those hearers in Corinth to get it, their eyes squinting and their heads cocked as they listened to the letter about glorying in weakness. Crucified in weakness, Paul wrote, but in that new way, raised through the whole experience because of My power.

Paul saw it. My precious Son was brought low so that they could be made new. Crucifixion is just another part of resurrection power. This insight changes everything. Then the frustrations, the beatings, the betrayals, the waiting, the imprisonment, the failures, all become part of that resurrection power. When I can use all those things for good, then my children finally become more than mere winners. "More than conquerors," as My scrappy Paul put it. Sure it was tough, but sometimes, after midnight, in a jail, I let him know how right he was.

Chapter 22

Acquiescing

Jesus (Luke 11; Luke 18; Matthew 26)

And he said to them, "Which of you who has a friend will go to him at midnight and say to him, 'Friend, lend me three loaves, for a friend of mine has arrived on a journey, and I have nothing to set before him'; and he will answer from within, 'Do not bother me; the door is now shut, and my children are with me in bed. I cannot get up and give you anything'? I tell you, though he will not get up and give him anything because he is his friend, *yet because of his impudence he will rise and give him whatever he needs.*

—Luke 11:5–8

And he told them a parable to the effect that they ought always to pray and not lose heart. He said, "In a certain city there was a judge who neither feared God nor respected man. And there was a widow in that city who kept coming to him and saying, 'Give me justice against my adversary.' For a while he refused, but afterward he said to himself, 'Though I neither fear God nor respect man, *yet because this widow keeps bothering me, I will give her justice, so that she will not beat me down by her continual coming.'"*

—Luke 18:1–5

Do you think that I cannot appeal to my Father, and he will at once send me more than twelve legions of angels? But how then should the Scriptures be fulfilled, that it must be so?" At that hour Jesus said to the crowds, "Have you come out as against a robber, with swords and clubs to capture me?"

—Matthew 26:53–55

I imagine that those who come after My first disciples will understand more. Some of them will have a lot of time in prisons to think about things. But My children with Me on earth now aren't getting it. So I tell them stories. They aren't perfect stories. I don't want them to be.

I tell them about a sleepy friend. It's midnight. The friend has been asleep for a long time. He is awakened by knocking and shouting. His neighbor needs bread.

No way. The friend says. I am in deep sleep. Everything is locked up. We can talk in the morning.

But this neighbor just keeps knocking, keeps shouting. Obnoxious. On and on and on. Finally the friend relents. He gives in. Why? Because the neighbor is relentless, untiringly persistent. No shame. He has that quality.

I'm teaching them about prayer. Their faces still look lost.

I tell them another story. I want the story to be disturbing. I want the story to be one they go back to again and again, turning it over and over like a strange coin, trying to figure it out.

It is a story about a corrupt, self-serving judge. This judge doesn't care about God or about his fellow citizens or about anything. He has the power.

The poor widow has no power. She asks the judge for help.

Forget about it. It's not going to happen.

She keeps bothering him, over and over and over. It is a survival trick of the helpless—to be annoying. What else can she do?

So the judge gives in. He allows her to win, not because he is good or cares about her at all or cares about God. She is just persistent, irritatingly persistent.

I want them to understand about prayer, about life. I don't want them to lose heart. I stare at their faces.

They are baffled. "A corrupt judge? Are you saying a corrupt judge is like God?" At least they are listening.

Yes, don't give up. Keep mulling it over. He lets the widow win. Keep puzzling. God will let you win, but sometimes you have to knock for a long time first. There's a reason for that.

They don't get it yet. I watch them struggle with it, their faces pinched, their eyes looking off in the distance in incomprehension.

Later, it becomes even harder for them to understand how life really goes.

In My darkest time I let the oppressors win. I didn't have to. I could have called thousands of angels to My side to stop that handful of soldiers. I made a point to tell My disciples this. I could have done a lot of things. I didn't lose My life. I gave it. So I let the others do the trapping, the whipping, and the nailing.

What does it mean to win or to lose? They will eventually see that there is more going on. They will see that sometimes people *let* you win, don't they? There may be some other reason for the fight.

How do you know when to fight and when to lose? That is the journey of life. The answer is simple. You fight and hold on when love tells you to fight and hold on, and you give in and lose when love tells you to give in and lose. Sometimes you need more persistence to give in than to hold on. Sometimes you don't.

I am always hoping they will begin to see—I won't give up on them. The Roman centurion saw it, a little, when he directed My execution. He had the power; he had the command. He knew how to win, but he was drawn to something more. It's always there—it is. That something more, that something beyond winning and losing.

"You saved others; why can't You save Yourself?"

It is the faces of the ones I love the most that hurt the most. The shocked face of Peter, with all his confidence burned away. John looking as though he has been run over. My mom.

My mom, who stands there looking at me, her little boy, twisting and struggling with every breath. She's so brave. The soldiers just wanted to get done for the day, but every second feels like a lifetime for her. It is such a terrible thing for a mother to watch her own child die a slow death by torture, and she knows that she can do nothing about it.

But there is something worse. Think of My Heavenly Father, who watches His special child die such a brutal death, and He *can* do something about it. In an instant. But He chooses not to. He chooses to lose. That is the real sacrifice.

It risks everything, doing things this way. The question arises—what if they don't get it? What if the world just thinks in its simple, linear way? What if the world just stands and gloats and insists that brutality and the show of force wins again, that deceit and conniving triumphs again? Goodness once again gets nailed to the wall. The people walk by, and they just snicker.

It is the risk I am willing to take. I will lose for them. I know that deep down beneath the cynicism is that better nature, that secret well, buried under the muck of experience and training from others. There is something there, if only they could see it once again. Losing may be the only real way to bring that fresh water to the surface, so I choose to lose. Here on this Cross.

Chapter 23

Acknowledging

The Outsider (Matthew 15:21–28)

And Jesus went away from there and withdrew to the district of Tyre and Sidon. And behold, a Canaanite woman from that region came out and was crying, "Have mercy on me, O Lord, Son of David; my daughter is severely oppressed by a demon." But he did not answer her a word. And his disciples came and begged him, saying, "Send her away, for she is crying out after us." He answered, "I was sent only to the lost sheep of the house of Israel." But she came and knelt before him, saying, "Lord, help me." And he answered, "It is not right to take the children's bread and throw it to the dogs." *She said, "Yes, Lord, yet even the dogs eat the crumbs that fall from their masters' table." Then Jesus answered her, "O woman, great is your faith! Be it done for you as you desire."* And her daughter was healed instantly.

—Matthew 15:21–28

This isn't just about her. I want them all to understand, so I took the position of my followers so they could see how it sounds. She is a foreigner, not one of our kind, not speaking our language, not looking like us. She is loud and way too pushy. She doesn't know the law and the prophets. They want to send her away, with all her incessant pleading for her daughter. So I say what they are all thinking. I was sent for our kind of people, who looked like us and acted like us. I can see them nod their heads.

But I watched her. At home she had been witnessing her daughter distorted in pain, just as my own mother will soon watch Me being tortured in agony.

And she won't give up. Yes, she is dramatic. She gets down on her knees in front of everyone. It is for her daughter. "Help me," she says with her eyes and her voice. This is her child. She grabs My hand. Everyone is quiet for just a moment, with the dust and the sun and the dryness.

I speak the words my followers are all thinking. It is not right to give to the dogs what was meant for the children. It was My time to be with My people, who spoke like I spoke and grew up like I grew up. That was enough, and even true in a certain way.

It's always the risk teachers must take. What will she do? After such words, she could quit and walk away. I watch her mull over the options, like grinding wheat. It is all on her face. She is relentless out of love—her love for her child. *Come on. You can do it.* This is the moment she might get up dejected, turn away, and leave. *Let's see what you are made of.*

"The righteous shall live by faithfulness." She doesn't know much, but she knows who to come to. She knows to keep plodding, to keep knocking. The rejection of the group, even the knowing roll of the eyes as they look at each other—it doesn't matter. She loves her daughter. She won't give up. She won't let Me go until I bless her.

Way to go. Way to go. She takes the initiative and reframes the scene. Forget about the crowd. She responds with her chin jutted out. She says even the dogs get the crumbs from the table. She's not giving up. She's not getting off her knees.

She sees My smile. I relent. She wins the argument. I tell her that her faith is great, her dogged trust in spite of the circumstances. Healing has come.

I watch the disciples. Do they get it? I lost. I let her win. They look at Me like deer startled and confused, surrounded by dogs. She is an important witness to them, but they don't yet even realize it. I spoke the way I did for her, but I also spoke the way I did for them.

Don't they see that My Father has often tested His children and then yielded? Haven't they read the law and the prophets?

Chapter 24

Yielding

Moses (Numbers 13–14; Exodus 17)

And the Lord said to Moses, "How long will this people despise me? And how long will they not believe in me, in spite of all the signs that I have done among them? I will strike them with the pestilence and disinherit them, and I will make of you a nation greater and mightier than they." But Moses said to the Lord, "Then the Egyptians will hear of it, for you brought up this people in your might from among them, and they will tell the inhabitants of this land. They have heard that you, O Lord, are in the midst of this people. For you, O Lord, are seen face to face, and your cloud stands over them and you go before them, in a pillar of cloud by day and in a pillar of fire by night. Now if you kill this people as one man, then the nations who have heard your fame will say, 'It is because the Lord was not able to bring this people into the land that he swore to give to them that he has killed them in the wilderness.' And now, please let the power of the Lord be great as you have promised, saying, 'The Lord is slow to anger and abounding in steadfast love, forgiving iniquity and transgression, but he will by no means clear the guilty, visiting the iniquity of the fathers on the children, to the third and the fourth generation.' *Please pardon the iniquity of this people, according to the greatness of your steadfast love, just as you have forgiven this people, from Egypt until now." Then the Lord said, "I have pardoned, according to your word.*

—Numbers 14:11–20

The Amalekites came and attacked the Israelites at Rephidim. Moses said to Joshua, *"Choose some of our men and go out to fight the Amalekites.* Tomorrow I will stand on top of the hill with the staff of God in my hands." So Joshua fought the Amalekites as Moses had ordered, and Moses, Aaron and Hur went to the top of the hill.

—Exodus 17:8–10 NIV

Moses was My law giver. He wasn't stupid. He wondered why I told the people all they had to do was to stand still at the crossing of the Red Sea. I told him I would fight for them. And I did fight for them. The finest army in the ancient world, the great Egyptian force, destroyed in a moment, destroyed by their own willfulness and pride.

But then, not too long after that, once they were in the wilderness, they had to deal with the troublesome Amalekites. The Amalakites lived in the wilderness. They knew the wilderness. The Hebrew people did not.

The Amalakites used guerilla tactics, coming from behind, killing the weak and the feeble. The Hebrew people were not accustomed to those badlands, nor to that kind of fighting. As slaves, they hadn't handled weapons for hundreds of years. Moses saw all this. He wanted to know why I just didn't eliminate the Amalakites the way I eliminated Pharaoh's mighty army. It wouldn't be hard for me. He knew I could do it.

But the Hebrew people had to learn to fight again. Moses understood. They had been pressed down, enslaved, spiritually cursed for so many generations—they had to find their grit again. They had to stop blaming people, particularly Moses. They had to dig deep down in the face of pressure, grit their teeth, and stop depending on someone else to fight for them.

This is one of the ways I have for My people to grow. It is one of the ways of life. My oaks grow strong under mighty winds, and My diamonds develop under pressure. And it had to be a little harder for them. A battle fought uphill makes one stronger than a battle fought downhill.

Moses slowly, quietly, began to understand. He didn't complain to Me about My directions, though he could have.

Yes, I was rough with Moses at times. I was working to make him understand. The good teacher bends to the level of his students. Often, a good teacher gives a student problems, not answers. A good teacher has to make the student work a bit.

Moses pushed on me at other times. Like the time when the people whined and complained about how big the people were in the Promised Land, how they wanted another leader, and how they wanted to go back to Egypt. Still the slave mentality. Still blaming others, still idealizing a past that never was, still finding a way to retreat. So little grit.

So I told Moses I would disinherit them and then make Moses a great nation. I wanted to see what Moses was made of. Moses still didn't understand the dance of severity and mercy and passionate love—why I would even say such a thing. He still didn't see the strands of human behavior that would lead through generations to incredible, deep heartache. On the other hand, the right choices could lead to a turn to the wondrous in times to come. He didn't think about the fact that past and future are the same to me, that I am not subject to time. He forgot that I am the one who invented time.

So Moses pushed back. His reasons were rudimentary. He said the Egyptians would assume I was not able to bring the people to the Promised Land. He reminded Me of My own words, that I am slow to anger. As though I had forgotten what I had told him, as though I didn't know what the Egyptians would say. He thought his arguments would sway Me, and I would pardon the people.

Way to go, Moses. He pressed on, challenging Me, trying to win an argument with Me, refusing the plum I had dangled before him, the promise he alone would be the great nation—the fame, the power, the legacy. I was so proud of him.

Then I let him win. I let him know I relented. With all his meager resources, he came back at Me, pressing Me, arguing with Me, doing his best to come up with reasons to convince Me of his limited understanding of mercy. He comprehended so little. He may not have been happy at the time, but for Me, it was one of his finest moments. He understood a little bit more, that I am a God who will give in for My special ones. In certain circumstances, I will resist and then relent. He even understood a bit more why I didn't do everything for My precious people, that sometimes they had to learn to fight.

In fact sometimes I will even let them fight with Me, like a father rough-housing with his little child. It can teach them so much. They can learn to take a bruise or two, to find strength they never thought they had, to learn about limits, to learn the right way to be what is so important—relentless. Abraham before Moses also learned he could press Me, and he learned when to stop.

Chapter 25

Deferring

Abraham (Genesis 18)

So the men turned from there and went toward Sodom, but Abraham still stood before the Lᴏʀᴅ. Then Abraham drew near and said, "Will you indeed sweep away the righteous with the wicked? Suppose there are fifty righteous within the city. Will you then sweep away the place and not spare it for the fifty righteous who are in it? Far be it from you to do such a thing, to put the righteous to death with the wicked, so that the righteous fare as the wicked! Far be that from you! Shall not the Judge of all the earth do what is just?" And the Lᴏʀᴅ said, "If I find at Sodom fifty righteous in the city, I will spare the whole place for their sake."

Abraham answered and said, "Behold, I have undertaken to speak to the Lord, I who am but dust and ashes. Suppose five of the fifty righteous are lacking. Will you destroy the whole city for lack of five?" And he said, "I will not destroy it if I find forty-five there." Again he spoke to him and said, "Suppose forty are found there." He answered, "For the sake of forty I will not do it." Then he said, "Oh let not the Lord be angry, and I will speak. Suppose thirty are found there." He answered, "I will not do it, if I find thirty there." He said, "Behold, I have undertaken to speak to the Lord. Suppose twenty are found there." He answered, "For the sake of twenty I will not destroy it." *Then he said, "Oh let not the Lord be angry, and I will speak again but this once. Suppose ten are found there." He answered, "For the sake of ten I will not destroy it."* And the L<small>ORD</small> went his way, when he had finished speaking to Abraham, and Abraham returned to his place.

—Genesis 18:22–33

I treated him like a friend. I told him what I was going to do. But I was testing him too. The people in those cities were killing each other, raping each other, robbing each other, withholding good from those in desperate need. It was a horrible downward spiral that would infect so much. What would Abraham say when I told him?

He knows so little. He doesn't even understand the complexity of his own destiny, what would happen if I don't come with severity. He doesn't see that My severity is a kindness. He doesn't see the dance of things that will happen, the mix of DNA, the destruction of his own line, the coming of Moses, David, of Jesus, the interplay of the seen and unseen, the inevitable consequences of this degree of wickedness, the connections that have implications for thousands of years and billions of people.

But Abraham has a touch of mercy; he thought about his own nephew and their friends. I like that about him. When I told him what I was going to do, he challenged Me. He didn't want to. His motives, as always, were mixed. In many ways he is a scaredy-cat, lying about his wife to protect his own skin, maneuvering his way through his hostile world. I had to smile as I watched him build up enough nerve to challenge Me.

Good. "What if there were fifty righteous people there?" he asks. He uses the word *righteous* as if he knows what it means. Good. Go ahead and press Me, Abraham. Then he lectures Me on what is right. I am pleased.

He is not a naturally brave man, My Abraham, but he presses on. This takes real courage. What if there were forty-five people that are "righteous"? He's trying to speak My language, or so he thinks. I wait a bit, let him know how serious this challenge is. Then I relent.

This is one reason he is My friend. He pushes further, using the only language he knows, the language of the market, as though he is making a deal with Me, a bargain. Forty people, thirty people, twenty people—he feels a twisting in the pit of his stomach. He has been so rash. I give in. Ten people. I let him understand that he has talked Me into it, this precious friend with his little drop of understanding of mercy and justice, the understanding I gave him. This understanding is growing each year he lives, facing frustration after frustration with Sarah, obstacle after obstacle, with no evidence of progeny on the horizon.

He has won. He has challenged his own understanding of Me, and he has won. He doesn't comprehend yet about losing, but he will. He has it in him. He let Lot win, let Lot take the best land, even though he himself had the power to take it. He was the leader, the uncle, the elder. Everything in his time would say he gets to choose. But he relented. He let the lesser feel as though he was the winner. This kind of realization doesn't happen in a day. But if anything at all, I am patient and persistent—especially about "losing" for my children.

He doesn't understand much of this yet—only that somehow he bartered mercy for the city. But his descendants through time will understand a bit more. Even his grandson will understand a little more, though he will have to go through his own fight.

Chapter 26

Losing

Jacob (Genesis 32)

And Jacob was left alone. And a man wrestled with him until the breaking of the day. When the man saw that he did not prevail against Jacob, he touched his hip socket, and Jacob's hip was put out of joint as he wrestled with him. Then he said, "Let me go, for the day has broken." But Jacob said, "I will not let you go unless you bless me." And he said to him, "What is your name?" And he said, "Jacob." Then he said, *"Your name shall no longer be called Jacob, but Israel, for you have striven with God and with men, and have prevailed."* Then Jacob asked him, "Please tell me your name." But he said, "Why is it that you ask my name?" And there he blessed him. So Jacob called the name of the place Peniel, saying, "For I have seen God face to face, and yet my life has been delivered." The sun rose upon him as he passed Penuel, limping because of his hip.

—Genesis 32:24–31

Of course I let him win. There in the night, he was fighting so much. In the end, he was fighting who he was. Of course he had made stupid mistakes—cheating his brother, his father, besting his uncle. He thought everything was a payment. If I did something for him, he would do something for Me. He has had night encounters with Me before. He didn't understand the stairway to heaven, not at all.

So we fought in the night. I knew how hard it was. I pushed him just enough, just to the point of exhaustion. Again and again. He needed to see what he was made of. I have to hand it to him. He had grit. He kept pushing, even when he didn't have any strength left. So the night went on, and we wrestled. I pressed him until he was almost defeated. Then I let him press Me until I was almost defeated. Then I pushed back again. Back and forth. For him, each minute felt like an hour.

People try to judge all things by their little tiny raindrop of experience. Jacob will think about this fight for the rest of his life. He doesn't understand much more than his grandfather, poor fellow. Wrestling is one of the ways I help life grow. It's the weak chicken pecking away and hatching out of its shell—you can't help the little thing. It's the butterfly straining to be born from the chrysalis, working life into its own wings in the process. It's the athletes pushing their muscles beyond their limits—or else the muscles won't grow. It's often the same with faith. To win without a struggle is to win without growth. There is more blessing for Jacob in the wrestling than in the victory.

When the ever-present thief robs a person in life, the person sometimes turns and blames Me. At times a person's own foolishness brings destruction. The center of My heart is forgiveness, but I won't stop all the hurts and disappointments in life. I didn't cause the hurt, but I won't stop it. Struggle is simply one of the ways I can develop the most important thing—the heart.

It's also one of the ways I am able to show affection, like a father wrestling with a child. Grappling is especially helpful when people have difficulty understanding anything else. Isn't it true? If I really love someone, I cannot deprive them of difficulties, can I? Not in this life.

My Jacob is learning. "I won't let you go unless you bless Me." He is learning not to lose heart. He is learning to knock and keep on knocking. He is learning to persist when the resistance goes on and on. He is learning that instead of letting go, there are times to grasp even harder—to be relentless.

It isn't hard for Me to enter his experience. I created it. The sweat, the heat, the straining of the muscles, the pressure of the elbow on the neck, the smell of his breath, the night air, the sound of the insects, even the ache of his shoulders when he could push no more. I understand.

Jacob didn't really know who he was wrestling. I touched his hip so he would remember Me. There's a cost to a fight. I'm proud of him. He didn't give up. I asked him to let Me go. He refused, pushing, pressing, insistent, grasping, clinging. I pressed back, always to the border of what he could handle. He wanted a blessing. Good old Jacob, wheeler-dealer Jacob. He makes Me smile.

So I ask him his name, there in the dark before the dawn. He has to say his own name—to face who he is. It took him a long time to say it, but he finally does. Jacob—the Hebrew for overreacher, supplanter, cheater. I take some time for it all to sink in, there in the dark, the light showing on the rim of the horizon. He really couldn't see My face, My approval.

So I give him a new name. I say it to his face, though he can't make out Mine in the dark. The name is special—it means he fought with Me and with men, and he won. He prevailed over God. Jacob the supplanter is now Israel the fighter. And because he is a fighter, he is a winner. The name Israel will echo through all time, reminding my people again and again that I gave Jacob the dignity of wrestling with Me, and then I let him win.

He has prevailed. A small inkling of what I was doing continues to seep in as he limps at dawn to meet the brother that hated him, the one he has fought with his entire life.

I have been losing for a long time. I could have stopped Adam and Eve, but they understood so little about love. I couldn't force them to love Me. I could have intervened so easily, but I let Myself be betrayed, beaten by the angel who hated Me. They didn't realize the cost for Me then or the cost for them now. The snake made Me look like a loser, but that is a part of love too.

One day they will understand more, but it will take time, a lot of time. In one sense, love is all about losing.

Capitulating

Child

Only five years old. Not a baby anymore. My little one is ready to wrestle right here in the living room. Sometimes it breaks my heart to see that fierce tiny posture and that expression of toughness, along with a serious intention to leap on me. As big as a mouse. Such a slight body, such skinny arms, so much of the world to face. So much that isn't known.

My small wrestler jumps on me, and I push back. A little desirable difficulty will help, a little more resistance. My wife leaves the room, with a shake of her head, still not approving of all the tussling.

My child groans and presses to the limit, so I groan as I push back. Retreating, and then on me again. That's the way. Show a little pluck.

I'm on my knees. I pick my small-fry up, and then—the slow-motion throwdown to the carpet. It's a jolt. A shocked look comes on my young one's face, but I cradle the tiny body just a bit so that it is not too rough. No cry comes out. The face of my opponent darkens in determination.

Now this insistent sprout bounces off the sofa and is at me again. Way to go. It almost brings tears to my eyes, this persistence. You will need that, my little one. Be relentless.

We push each other again. I shove back firmly. I growl, beckoning, challenging.

Then the rush, and I allow myself to be pushed down. Now I am on the bottom, and I allow my wrists to be compelled toward the floor. I resist. Our arms are suspended in the air, straining for something, developing those little muscles with every moment. Slowly, slowly, not too quickly, I allow the impossible. My own arms are being pushed to the floor.

This small face in front of me doesn't show understanding now. But years later, decades later, it might. A resilient spirit is one of the greatest gifts I can give. There. My arms finally submit to being pressed to the floor.

When I am pinned, my own offspring is stunned and exhausted. With a crow of victory, the match is done. A crow of victory—that precious pint-sized cry that twists my heart. It was harder than imagined, but the indestructible father has actually been beaten. Yes, I have lost the fight, for the sake of my own little one.

So come on, my child, let's see what you are made of.

Appendix A

Scripture Verses to Feed On
Being Relentless

Then he said, "Let me go, for the day has broken." But Jacob said, *"I will not let you go unless you bless me."* —Genesis 32:26

It is the LORD who goes before you. He will be with you; he will not leave you or forsake you. *Do not fear or be dismayed."* —Deuteronomy 31:8

Have I not commanded you? *Be strong and courageous. Do not be frightened, and do not be dismayed*, for the LORD your God is with you wherever you go." —Joshua 1:9

Behold, if the river is turbulent *he is not frightened; he is confident* though Jordan rushes against his mouth. —Job 40:23

Even though I walk through the valley of the shadow of death, *I will fear no evil, for you are with me*; your rod and your staff, they comfort me. —Psalm 23:4

He will not be afraid of evil tidings; His heart is steadfast, trusting in the LORD. *His heart is established; He will not be afraid*, until he sees *his desire* upon his enemies. —Psalm 112:7–8 NKJV

Your will to live can sustain you when you are sick, but if you lose it, your last hope is gone. Intelligent people are always eager and ready to learn. Do you want to meet an important person? Take a gift and it will be easy. —Proverbs 18:14–16 GNT

If you faint in the day of adversity, Your strength is small. —Proverbs 24:10 NKJV

The godly may trip seven times, but they will get up again. But one disaster is enough to overthrow the wicked. —Proverbs 24:16 NLT

And *though the Lord give you the bread of adversity and the water of affliction, yet your Teacher will not hide himself anymore*, but your eyes shall see your Teacher. —Isaiah 30:20

I will let you be like a log covered with sharp spikes. You will grind and crush every mountain and hill until they turn to dust. —Isaiah 41:15 CEV

He will not grow faint or be discouraged till he has established justice in the earth. —Isaiah 42:4

But the Lord God helps me; therefore I have not been disgraced; therefore *I have set my face like a flint.* —Isaiah 50:7

Beat your plowshares into swords, and your pruning hooks into spears: *let the weak say, I am strong.* —Joel 3:10 KJV

Though the fig tree should not blossom, nor fruit be on the vines, the produce of the olive fail and the fields yield no food, the flock be cut off from the fold and there be no herd in the stalls, *yet I will rejoice in the Lord; I will take joy in the God of my salvation.* —Habakkuk 3:17–18

In this godless world *you will continue to experience difficulties. But take heart!* I've conquered the world. —John 16:33 *The Message*

But *none of these things move me*, neither count I my life dear unto myself, so that I might finish my course with joy. —Acts 20:24 KJV

No, in all these things we are *more than conquerors* through him who loved us. —Romans 8:37

Love never gives up. —1 Corinthians 13:4 *The Message*

So, my dear brothers and sisters, *be strong and immovable*. Always work enthusiastically for the Lord, for you know that nothing you do for the Lord is ever useless. —1 Corinthians 15:58 NLT

Be on your guard; *stand firm in the faith; be courageous; be strong.* Do everything in love. —1 Corinthians 16:13–14 NIV

Now thanks *be* to God *who always leads us in triumph in Christ.* —2 Corinthians 2:14 NKJV

And let us not grow weary of doing good, for in due season we will reap, *if we do not give up.* —Galatians 6:9

Finally, *be strong in the Lord* and in the strength of his might. —Ephesians 6:10

Fight the good fight of the faith. —1 Timothy 6:12

Don't drag your feet. Be like those who *stay the course with committed faith* and then get everything promised to them. —Hebrews 6:12 *The Message*

But you need to stick it out, staying with God's plan so you'll be there for the promised completion. —Hebrews 10:36 *The Message*

But *we are not quitters* who lose out. Oh, no! *We'll stay with it and survive,* trusting all the way. —Hebrews 10:39 *The Message*

God is educating you; *that's why you must never drop out*. He's treating you as dear children. This trouble you're in isn't punishment; *it's training*, the normal experience of children. —Hebrews 12:7 *The Message*

Beloved, *do not be surprised* at the fiery trial when it comes upon you to test you, as though something strange were happening to you. —1 Peter 4:12

This calls for patient endurance on the part of the people of God who keep his commands and remain faithful to Jesus. —Revelation 14:12 NIV

Appendix B

Scripture Verses to Feed On
Relenting for the Sake of the Other Person

Then he said, "Your name shall no longer be called Jacob, but Israel, *for you have striven with God* and with men, *and have prevailed.*" —Genesis 32:28

But *with you there is forgiveness*, that you may be feared. —Psalm 130:4

Do you think that I cannot appeal to my Father, and *he will at once send me more than twelve legions of angels?* But how then should the Scriptures be fulfilled, that it must be so? —Matthew 26:53

I am the good shepherd. The good shepherd *lays down his life* for the sheep. —John 10:11

Just as the Father knows me and I know the Father; and *I lay down my life* for the sheep. —John 10:15

For this reason the Father loves me, because *I lay down my life* that I may take it up again. No one takes it from me, but *I lay it down of my own accord. I have authority to lay it down*, and I have authority to take it up again. This charge I have received from my Father. —John 10:17–18

He who did not spare his own Son *but gave him up for us all*, how will he not also with him graciously *give us all things*? —Romans 8:32

God is faithful, and *he will not let you be tempted beyond your ability*, but with the temptation *he will also provide the way of escape, that you may be able to endure it.* —1 Corinthians 10:13

[Christ's love] does not insist on its own way. —1 Corinthians 13:5

Love bears all things, believes all things, hopes all things, endures all things. —1 Corinthians 13:7

You are familiar with the generosity of our Master, Jesus Christ. Rich as he was, *he gave it all away for us*—in one stroke he became poor and we became rich. —2 Corinthians 8:9 *The Message*

For *he was crucified in weakness*. —2 Corinthians 13:4

And one of the elders said to me, "Weep no more; behold, the Lion of the tribe of Judah, the Root of David, has conquered, so that he can open the scroll and its seven seals." And between the throne and the four living creatures and among the elders *I saw a Lamb standing, as though it had been slain*. —Revelation 5:5–6

About Taylor Field and
Graffiti Community Ministry

Graffiti Community Ministry started in a storefront forty years ago. Now it works to express God's love in tangible ways for thousands each year through Graffiti 2 in the South Bronx, Graffiti 3 in Brooklyn, Gotta Serve in Long Island, and Graffiti Ministries Coney Island. Graffiti has affiliates in places such as Baltimore, Syracuse, and Buffalo. It has fostered and supported more than sixty new churches while acting as mother church, aunt church, or grandmother church. It also partners with a number of other ministries in New York City in a commitment to do the small thing in order to serve the unserved. For more information, contact Graffiti Community Ministry at 205 E. 7th Street, New York, NY 10009, (212) 473-0044, or go to graffitichurch.org. To learn more about Graffiti's Upside Down Training, go to upsidedownlife.org.

This book of biblical reflections is a result of more than forty years of work with those who are homeless or in difficult situations.

For more than thirty years Taylor Field has served as the pastor director of Graffiti Church and Community Ministries in New York City, where he has been recognized for his church and community ministry. Working with more than ten thousand people a year, Graffiti Community Ministries serves and empowers children, youth, and adults in the Lower East Side of Manhattan. Taylor has a PhD from Gateway Seminary and an MDiv from Princeton Seminary. He is the author of *The Wayward Way, Upside-Down Leadership, Upside-Down Freedom, Upside-Down Devotion, Mercy Street,* and *Squat.* He works together with his wife Susan Field, and they have two married children and five grandchildren.

If you enjoyed this book, will you consider sharing the message with others?

Let us know your thoughts at info@newhopepublishers.com. You can also let the author know by visiting or sharing a photo of the cover on our social media pages or leaving a review at a retailer's site. All of it helps us get the message out!

Twitter.com/NewHopeBooks

Facebook.com/NewHopePublishers

Instagram.com/NewHopePublishers

————

New Hope® Publishers, Ascender Books, Iron Stream Books, and New Hope Kidz are imprints of Iron Stream Media,
which derives its name from Proverbs 27:17,
"As iron sharpens iron, so one person sharpens another."

This sharpening describes the process of discipleship, one to another. With this in mind, Iron Stream Media provides a variety of solutions for churches, ministry leaders, and nonprofits ranging from in-depth Bible study curriculum and Christian book publishing to custom publishing and consultative services. Through the popular Life Bible Study and Student Life Bible Study brands, ISM provides web-based full-year and short-term Bible study teaching plans as well as printed devotionals, Bibles, and discipleship curriculum.

For more information on ISM and New Hope Publishers,
please visit

IronStreamMedia.com

NewHopePublishers.com